The Practice of
Foreign Language Teaching

The Practice of Foreign Language Teaching

Second Edition

Wasyl Cajkler and Ron Addelman

David Fulton Publishers
2 Park Square, Milton Park, Abingdon, Oxon OX14 4RN

First edition published in Great Britain by David Fulton Publishers 1992
Transferred to digital printing

David Fulton Publishers is an imprint of the Taylor & Francis Group, an informa business

Copyright © Wasyl Cajkler and Ron Addelman 2000

Note: The right of Wasyl Cajkler and Ron Addelman to be identified as the authors of this work has been asserted by them in accordance with the Copyright, Designs and Patents Act 1988.

British *Library Cataloguing in Publication Data*
A catalogue record for this book is available from the British Library.

ISBN 1–85346–570–4

Typeset by Textype Typesetters, Cambridge

Contents

For Eda and Mary

Acknowledgements

We wish to thank all the many teachers who have contributed to materials used in this book, either directly or indirectly by sharing ideas. Particular thanks are due to former Tameside colleagues: Karen Hanks, Sally Bowden, John Alder, John Blake, Lynne Taylor, Brenda Harvey and Keith Haughan. We also thank Fiona White, Julie Norton, Anne Coquin, Carmela Cuthbertson, Julie Thomson, and Martin White. Also Rachel Whatley for her work on the manuscript for the first edition, some of which has been carried forward. The authors are grateful to Rachel James for a number of illustrations, to Peter Jordan for some of the examples of classroom organisation and to Stephen Cajkler for his occasional contributions to the chapter about sixth form language learning.

The authors and publishers would like to thank the following for permission to include examples of materials: Simon & Schuster Publishers, Somerset Thinking Skills Course, SNCF Railways, and Presidenza del Consiglio dei Ministri. We also thank Leicestershire Multicultural Resources Centre for the story of Lord Rex, a French version of which we have used in our teaching. Every effort has been made to trace copyright owners and to acknowledge contributions. If any omission has occurred we will be pleased to make the necessary acknowledgements in future printings.

Introduction

Like all authors, we want our book to be read and we have tried to produce a new edition which teachers will want to read and find useful. To achieve this, we have written it in such a manner that it should be accessible and easy to read. The chapters are, on the whole, self-contained, so that readers who are searching for information on only one aspect of teaching will not have to read the whole book to find it. Nevertheless the book is designed to present a unified approach. This leads on occasion to a repetition of ideas, which is not accidental. The various sections relate and refer to each other. We have not produced a comprehensive guide to modern language teaching: a short book such as this could not hope to do that.

The layout of the text is at times generous in its use of double spacing and indentation. We believe that hard-pressed teachers want to gain easy access to practical ideas. We must stress that we do not intend our solutions and suggestions to be taken as the only ones available. They are possibilities which we think have value. The index is also intended to lead readers to possible solutions to specific problems in various parts of the book.

The content of the book

The book deals mainly, but not solely, with the teaching of modern foreign languages. When discussing behavioural problems, it is general teaching skills and not foreign language methodology which are to the fore.

After the introduction the book is divided into seven sections. The section on pupils and teachers tackles general and modern languages issues from the perspectives of both learners and teachers, giving appropriate focus to their needs. The section on teaching and learning in the foreign language classroom considers various aspects of planning and organisation of lessons. The target language chapters are the practical nucleus of the book, giving as many examples as possible of maximising the use of the target language and helping pupils learn through relevant ways of handling grammar and vocabulary. The section on assessment, recording and reporting has been revised to incorporate developments in legislation and methodology in recent years. We have added new chapters on teaching advanced level students and on information technology. The concluding section discusses some coping strategies we have found that worked, including ideas on time management. We have both experienced the negative effects of stress and believe that a work concerned with the practical aspects of teaching should include at least a mention of the strategies we have found helpful.

The book was revised as the National Curriculum was undergoing its second revision. The impact of this will not emerge until some time after our date of publication. We are, however, convinced of the validity of the great bulk of the thinking in this book whatever the outcome of the revision may be.

Audiences

The audiences that we intended to write for are threefold: teachers who have recently entered the profession, student teachers soon to enter it and those who have been teaching for a number of years and may need timely reminders of things which were once second nature but have fallen into disuse or misuse. The age group we had in mind was, in the main, 11–16; but Chapter 10, specifically on teaching A Level students, should serve as an introduction to a topic which still receives far too little attention. We are not convinced that the methodological needs of older students are always very different from those of younger pupils. Many of the ideas and examples we have selected may be seen to be relevant to the needs of learners younger than 11.

Practicality

Above all this is a practical book. It does not cover every possible aspect of teaching. The experienced teacher will soon identify omissions, some but not all of which are deliberate. The last two decades have been a period of great change in education, though not necessarily in teaching methodology. Many of the methodological changes of that period had their seeds sown well before it. Teachers have had to internalise the implications of graded objectives, communicative approaches, GCSE, computer-assisted language learning, and National Curriculum statements of attainment. However, despite frequent changes in specifications, ideas for teaching have always been valued by reflective teachers. This book seeks to offer food for thought that will help teachers to deliver the courses they wish to teach well into the 21st century. We hope that teachers and would-be teachers will find in this book strategies, materials and advice which will save them time and labour. There is no copyright on ideas. We hope that they will used, adapted and improved upon by practising teachers.

Sources

In this book we draw on ideas and materials culled from our work together, our contacts with many colleagues in the profession, our readings, our work in Tameside schools, Greater Manchester and Cheshire and our observations in many classrooms throughout the UK over the last few years. We are indebted to Tameside Local Education Authority and the individual teachers who are acknowledged elsewhere for their permission to use their materials. There are undoubtedly countless other teachers whose work, though unacknowledged by name, has contributed to the ideas in the book.

Style

If we manage to put over our ideas in a simple and direct manner which readers can cope with and not find a hindrance as they look for answers to specific problems, that is elegance enough. Much of the discussion undertaken in preparation for the writing of this book has aimed at avoiding educational jargon, which proliferated in the late twentieth century. Despite our efforts we are sure that jargon has crept in. For this we apologise. The layout of the book has been designed so that readers can find their way through the brief theoretical sections to the examples which are at its heart. We have put some effort into reducing the theoretical content of the book to a minimum, attractive though we both find it to philosophise. Other works should be referred to for more detailed theoretical explanations. We surmise that teachers who refer to this work will do so principally for advice on practice, less on theory. Implications for the classroom are often explicitly identified.

Pupils and genders

In referring to learners we vary between calling them pupils, students, young people and learners, purely for the sake of variety. We have tended to avoid the term students (other than for post-16 learners). We had no easy solution to the dilemma of whether to refer to a teacher or a pupil as he, she, s/he, (s)he or he or she. Some of these alternatives we found clumsy. Readers will find that we use the term she or he to refer to either and should understand that we are referring to both genders whenever we use one of these terms unless the issue being discussed particularly relates to gender.

Which languages?

Our examples and ideas can apply to any language being taught. Though many of the materials are in French, we also draw on German, Italian, Spanish and, of course, English. Supporters of particular languages may well be offended by the proliferation of French in this work. We had to draw on the languages we felt strongest in. Our experience shows that materials and activities in one language can usually be easily adapted to work in another.

Realism

Another parameter which we tried to confine ourselves to was realism. Can we expect teachers to do this? Would we? People of all ages are more important than systems, no matter how efficient. Teachers, indeed all involved in education, are overwhelmed with administrative tasks imposed by government, local and national, and school management, all with the aim of improving the efficiency of the education system, but leading to a potential reduction of the time teachers can devote to teaching. We have tried to bear this in mind in our advice and expectations. Our reasons for this stance are unashamedly connected with realism, stress management and practicality.

Languages for all

One of the main implications of the advent of the National Curriculum was the extension of the age to which pupils have by law to learn a modern foreign language. Admittedly it will be possible from September 2000 for some pupils to stop studying modern foreign languages; but a significant number will continue. Through their involvement with pupils of all abilities after Year 9, teachers have experienced methodological difficulties of the type which we try to deal with in this book: classroom organisation, class management, selection of materials, assessment and recording of achievement, for example.

A partnership

When two people write a book, there are inevitably 'difficulties'. Some are stylistic. We have tried to eliminate glaring stylistic differences. It will not come as a shock to readers if we admit that we carved up the writing of the chapters between us, undertaking roughly half the book each. The ideas in the chapters were, however, shared, often to the extent of their being the result of a joint planning session to work out where we stood. We have tried to avoid philosophical and methodological differences. We both found the task of working together on this project enjoyable and rewarding, even though the time we devoted to it was sometimes costly. Readers will be able to judge whether or not our time was well spent.

Section 1: Pupils and teachers

Chapter 1

Being a pupil

Attitudes and motivation

We deal with children constantly at work and in our, perhaps, rare leisure hours, yet it is not difficult to forget what it feels like to be a child. Childhood pleasures, joys, pains and fears are similar to, but not the same as, those we experience in adulthood. We do not have the right to expect children to have the same sense of urgency about learning anything in the school context as teachers have to teach it. Children's attitudes to learning a foreign language, both positive and negative, are influenced by many factors: age, peer-group pressure, school ethos, home background attitudes, teachers' skills, the strong feeling that 'everyone' abroad speaks English, experience of travel abroad, job ambitions. More important than even these factors is the feeling that modern languages are the most difficult subject in the curriculum, offering pupils an opportunity to fail, to feel inadequate, to get it wrong. This must inevitably damage the self-esteem of many pupils, who, as they enter their teenage years already experience self-doubt and do not want more problems in their lives than they already have. So languages teachers have a big task on their hands. The most realistic approach teachers can take with this range of positive and negative factors in mind is to 'grow' their own attitudes in class and in school, using themselves, their teaching and inter-personal skills as the fertiliser for the pupils' desire to learn or to take part in the lesson. They should certainly not take it for granted that children will arrive in the classroom with a strong positive attitude to foreign language learning. It may even be helpful for teachers to adopt a critical attitude to the tasks and expectations they create in their classrooms: this may lead to a healthy questioning of the work they prepare and the schemes of work they follow.

It is possible to identify two basic types of motivation: intrinsic and extrinsic. Intrinsic motivation comes from within the individual. It does not need external stimuli to provoke it. A learner, whether it is a child obsessed with the computer or a pure physicist, may delight in learning for learning's sake. Many learners of all ages, however, need external stimuli, something or someone other than themselves to create the desire to learn or to work in any way. This is extrinsic motivation. It can be obtained by offering privileges, rewards, signs of approval, the promise (always fulfilled) of pleasant experiences. Bearing in mind the realism suggested above, it is wise to assume that the most prevalent type of motivation in the classroom will be extrinsic. This does not necessarily make the task of teaching a foreign language very difficult. Teaching is all about nurturing a culture which facilitates learning. It helps if one actually likes children; they can usually detect this and will, in many cases, work to please the teacher. Most children are motivated by their attitude to the teacher. They also have a need for fun and are easily bored. Younger pupils of both sexes can develop positive attitudes to foreign language learning if the experience is successful. Older pupils may consider that they are in school on sufferance; the older they get, the more they want to be out in what they consider the real world. Yet they can enjoy their work and even carry out tasks which may be considered in the cold light of day too young for them, if the relationship between pupils and teacher is right. Modern linguists often say theirs is one of the hardest subjects for which to create motivation. There is some truth in this, but we still have to find strategies to deal with this. The complex mixture of things which stimulate learning must lead to some 'investment' by pupils, no matter how modest.

Parental expectations can be a positive or a negative force in the child's learning. An able child's parents may have high expectations. In a mixed-ability class, teachers need to offer tasks which will meet such high expectations. Conversely, not all parents of children with learning difficulties encourage their children to learn or experience a foreign language.

Maslow's (1954) hierarchy of human needs stresses the importance of self-esteem and the esteem of other people. Learners need to get meaningful feedback from their teachers. If their teacher shows recognition, values what they do, what they achieve, most pupils will try to earn it. Perhaps the most powerful motivator is self-esteem. A pupil who is given tasks to do that make her feel good about herself, will make good progress.

Implications for the classroom

Fun is obtained from:

- smiles,
- language games,
- competitions which anyone can win,
- competitions which the 'best' can win,
- friendly jokes and quips,
- puzzles,
- problems to solve,
- making things,
- moving about,
- the unexpected,
- the unpredictable,
- the privilege of relaxing now and then,
- success in learning.

Motivators include:

- some kind of reward (time out, a fun activity, a comic to read, etc.);
- praise by peers;
- genuine, warm praise by the teacher;
- a special visitor;
- an attempt to show that tasks are relevant;
- a clear understanding of what the task ahead is (notes, target sheets, verbal explanation, work schedules);
- success in learning.

Pupils should start on the path of foreign language learning as early as possible. Primary school experiences appear to have a long-lasting effect on boys and girls. They create good work habits. It is worth exploring the possibility of links with local primary schools. Consideration of the work in many parts of the country, where opportunities for pupils to make an early start to their modern language learning are offered, leads to a conviction that positive attitudes to language learning, whatever the language, are implanted by an early start in the environment to which pupils have become accustomed over a number of years: their first school. The rapidly increasing number of primary language schemes around the UK endorses this view.

Be positive and offer an opportunity for all to succeed at a level which they think is worthwhile. Lessons or tasks which are about failing run the risk of causing long-term damage: resentment, demotivation, fear of failure, refusal to cooperate and loss of pupils' investment in their own learning.

Authentic materials and realia should be brought into the classroom where possible.

Native speakers are great motivators, particularly if pupils have prepared for the visit.

Create opportunities for other willing teachers to use the target language (the head teacher uses German in front of the whole school; a teacher comes into the classroom and speaks French).

Relationships

From the pupil's viewpoint, being in a school is first and foremost a matter of relationships: pupil–pupil, pupil–teacher, pupil–others. Peer-group relationships in the language classroom are fascinating and far from straightforward. As in the world outside of school, the languages classroom may not be an easy place for girls to be in, though often they excel in language learning. In mixed-ability classes, girls are conscious of boys who tease them and may be less than willing to 'perform' in the languages lesson because of it.

Boys tend to hog the hardware, such as computers, unless the teacher takes steps to encourage the girls. Boys who want to practise, to speak, to answer a question, to try at their homework may be ridiculed openly or surreptitiously by other boys trying to create an aggressive, supposedly masculine image by deriding hard-working pupils as 'keenoes'. Boys can also be attention-seeking and can dominate the classroom, even when the teacher thinks she is giving equal attention to girls and boys. Children can, however, be very community-conscious and tolerant. The able will help the less able; the class will support the pupil who has missed work through an absence; children spontaneously help each other with homework. Some teachers consciously establish a system of 'study buddies' to profit from this natural tendency in their pupils. By so doing they are merely formalising and approving what already happens. A study buddy must be trained to be sparing in her support in order to maintain the independence of the pupil assisted and to devote time to their own studies, which are, in fact, improved when they support a classmate. The best way to learn is to teach.

A language teacher most likely hopes to create a relaxed atmosphere in the classroom, one in which the pupils will be prepared to 'perform' if the class is engaged in oral work. This aim may be in conflict with the needs imposed by the discipline requirements of a particular group. The creation of an atmosphere of fear is not conducive to learning, though there is some evidence that some pressure can be formative, if it challenges pupils to reach their full potential. The role of the teacher will vary from that of authority figure to friend (but be careful!), to 'expert' to consultant, depending on the prevailing attitude in the group, the age of its members and the type of course which is being taught.

The picture of the world presented to learners should be a balanced one, so that stereotypes are avoided and all pupils are valued. Everyone needs to feel valued by others and OK about themselves. The teacher has a role in creating opportunities for both. It is a difficult area because it involves each pupil being given equal positive regard whatever their ethnic background, creed or colour. If they see a white middle-class world view dominating their activities, exercise books, textbooks, what message is this transmitting? What kind of motivation is it going to produce? It will certainly produce negative self-images for many pupils. A constant diet of steak and chips will not suit children who eat lentils, curried vegetables and rice and ought to be able to talk about it in the language they are learning. Appreciating pupils means not treating them as if they are all the same.

At school pupils come into contact with a range of 'others'. Younger pupils can meet older pupils who can be helpful or threatening, hopefully the former. Foreign nationals such as Foreign Languages Assistants (FLAs) can offer a temptation to 'have fun', have a chat in English or practise what has been learnt. Teachers other than the languages teachers rarely show any reaction to the foreign language.

Implications for the classroom

Older pupils can create materials for younger pupils, either in their own school or in the nearest primary school (games, comics, stories, readers). They can actually work with the younger pupils if it can be arranged. Remember that younger pupils will be critical of materials which look shoddy and may even be demotivated by them. Careful negotiation between teachers involved will be required. The very fact that they are creating materials for younger pupils has a strong potential to make pupils feel responsible, to want to produce accurate target language. There is a role for information and communications technology (ICT) applications here (see Chapter 11). An extension of this is the 'paired reading' approach which has been used for some years in primary schools, where older and younger readers are encouraged and trained to read together, to become reading partners. It could be older and younger children or, in the case of primary children learning to read English, children and parents.

Pair work can also be used to enable the more able to assist the less able or to give children of similar abilities a chance to undertake a task commensurate with their ability.

The languages lesson should not become a place of non-stop performance. Pupils in many classes will not be able to cope with more than short bursts of oral work. A lesson should contain a range of activities, develop a range of skills, approach the topic in hand from a variety of perspectives.

The teacher would be wise to take cognisance of intra-class relationships and plan with them in mind. It is worthwhile keeping an eye open to find out who are friends or enemies with whom, who likes sitting with or avoiding whom.

Avoid embarrassing pupils by forcing 'public' activities upon them. Reading aloud can be an ego-trip for the good reader and pure hell for others (including the teacher, who feels tempted to correct almost every word a poor reader utters). Performing role-plays in front of the class can similarly be counter-productive, unless the whole class feels involved, by being asked to react in some way, which will motivate rather than demotivate the performers. Some pupils, however, actually enjoy showing off. So long as the public activity is voluntary, no harm will be done.

It does no harm for pupils to realise that the teacher is human, has moods and can have expectations of herself (or himself). Openness, if used consciously, can enhance relationships without exposing the teacher to contempt bred by over-familiarity.

The non-language times can be important ones for the language learner. 'Time out' gives teachers time to talk in a different way with pupils. 'Home news' from teacher or pupils can equally help develop relationships which can be built up in the more academic moments.

Different abilities

All children benefit from the experience of learning a foreign language, whether as a means of developing new skills up to a high level or simply to extend their awareness that people in other countries communicate in a different way from their own. It is difficult to justify denying to any child the entitlement to a full curriculum. Parents have the right to expect that their children, whatever their abilities and skills, will have access to a wide range of learning experiences. Modern languages, as much as any area of the curriculum, offer the opportunity for success and fun at school. Teachers in the 1990s became increasingly aware of the range of abilities they were dealing with in their classrooms, whether in mixed ability or separate ability teaching environments. New forms of accreditation such as the Certificate of Achievement have been developed. Teachers have widened their awareness of differentiating their approach. The current understanding of the term 'special educational needs' extends from meeting the needs of our most able pupils through to dealing with temporary academic setbacks to children with a range of physical and learning needs.

A brief scan of learning needs reveals some of the types of need teachers have to meet:

- Emotional and Behavioural Difficulty (EBD)
- Moderate Learning Difficulty (MLD)
- Mild Learning Difficulty
- Specific Learning Difficulty (SpLD) equated with dyslexia
- Severe Learning Difficulty (SLD)
- Partially Hearing (PH)
- Visually Impaired (VI).

It is our belief that the majority of children with such needs have the right to learn a foreign language and will benefit from the experience educationally, socially and culturally. That does not mean that the teacher's task is straightforward. Certainly the teacher of children with learning difficulties of any kind can take nothing for granted. Some children have attention span and visual and mental focus problems; others do not easily acquire some concepts, though one has to stretch one's imagination a great deal to say that any child is incapable of acquiring any concepts, for concepts can range in complexity from the abstract grammatical points to a simple awareness of difference.

It is important to distinguish between short-term and long-term memory (see Figure 1.1). Very few children, even those with severe learning difficulties, have difficulty in retaining information in their long-term memory once the short-term memory has internalised the information. A teacher's ingenuity is stretched in the attempt to find ways of getting the information into the child's short-term memory, whose span is only a matter of seconds. In other words, getting the information in is far harder than keeping it in.

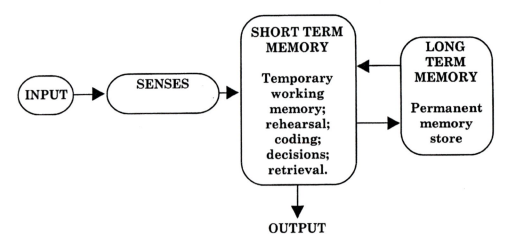

Figure 1.1

The traditional myth is that modern linguists stretch the able child but fail to offer a meaningful experience to less gifted children. All learners are entitled to expect that what they learn will provide them with all four language skills (listening, speaking, reading and writing (LSRW)) to the full extent of their ability. Able children in particular are stimulated by problem-solving, open-ended activities, tasks which they can carry out independently and those which allow them to use their imagination. They can work quickly; the teacher needs to supply them with extension materials which are not simply more of what they can already do. They benefit from occasionally working with others of similar ability and interests. They are also sometimes embarrassed by their own ability and may wish occasionally to work by themselves, where they will not be noticed. Children need targets to aim at which they feel are within their reach. So tasks should be set in a manner which is clearly understood by pupils and be designed on the principle of success not failure. Success will lead to pupils being prepared to invest more energy into their learning. Failure, on the other hand, reduces their willingness to invest time, effort and concentration.

Teachers too have expectations of their pupils. They affect all children either directly or indirectly. High expectations of some but not of others create an environment of care for some, neglect for others. The able and the less able child should feel that teachers expect them to do their best, to improve and to learn.

In the 1990s teachers grappled with the challenge of offering pupils of all abilities a course in modern language learning for the five years of secondary education. A range of commercial courses was developed and these have now been tried and tested. They include: *Avantage* (McNab 1992), *Route Nationale* (Briggs *et al.* 1992), *Spirale 1* (Jenkins and Jones 1991) and their German and Spanish equivalents. A new generation of course books includes courses devoted to the needs of learners with learning difficulties such as *Génial* (Elston *et al.* 1995), *Vital 1* (Corney and Buckby 1995), *OK! Stage 1* (Finnie 1993) and *OK! Stage 2* (Finnie and Cambier 1996), *Deutsch? Kein Problem!* (Brown *et al.* 1996). Teachers will evaluate such materials. Some more recently produced coursebooks are being introduced to challenge the courses developed in the late 1980s and early 1990s: *Équipe* (Bourdais *et al.* 1998), *Un Deux Trois* (Kavanagh and O'Connor 1999), for example.

Implications for the classroom

Able children should be given as many self-help strategies as possible, so that they have opportunities to:

- use a dictionary;
- construct sentences;
- build new sentences based on what has already been learnt;
- apply rules;
- spell accurately;
- use free-standing materials independently of teacher support;
- follow their individual reading programme and write their own book reviews;

- use a range of stylistic devices in their productive work;
- read a newspaper in the target language.

(But do not make the mistake of neglecting the able child for the sake of giving more time to the others.)

The map and activities we give here were based on the Somerset Thinking Skills materials (Blagg *et al.* 1988).

Figure 1.2

Schatzinsel

1. *Verfassen Sie eine kurze Beschreibung der Insel.* (Write a brief description of the island.)
2. *Schreiben Sie zwanzig Fragen, die man stellen könnte, um herauszufinden, wo der Schatz auf der Insel versteckt wurde.* (Write 20 questions which could be asked to find out where the treasure has been hidden on the island.)

   zum Beispiel: Ist der Schatz hinter den Baümen?
   Gibt es Baüme in der Nähe des Schatzes?

Folgende Ausdrücke können Ihnen nützlich sein: (You may find the following expressions useful:)

im Norden		im Süden		im Westen			im Osten
links	rechts	in der Mitte	hinter	vor	unter	über	in	auf
amStrand	die Hutten	die Palmen		der Pier	das Boot		die Felsen

3. *Wählen Sie auf der Karte ein passendes Versteck für den Schatz aus. Von Ihren ursprünglich zwanzig Fragen wählen Sie fünf, die Ihnen helfen könnten, den Schatz zu entdecken, wenn man, davon ausgeht, dass Sie vom Kai abfahren.* (On the map select a suitable hiding place for the treasure. From your original 20 questions select five which could lead you to find the treasure, assuming you were setting off from the quay.)
4. *Begründen Sie, warum Sie dieses Versteck gewählt haben. Bedenken Sie die verschiedenen Umstände, die Ihre Auswahl beeinflussen sollten.* (Write your reasons for your choice of hiding place. Think of the various conditions which should have affected your choice.)

Any materials which require children with learning difficulties to read or take in information with their eyes should be easy on the eye and characterised by:

- thick borders around worksheets;
- limited information/content at any one time (do not cram the page or the board);
- clearly printed words, capital and lower case letters should be in the correct case to avoid confusion;
- attractive layout;
- highlighting of key points (headings, arrows, underlining, boxes and different typefaces);
- short sentences;
- clear, easily-deciphered pictures;
- clear symbols or codes (if too sophisticated, for example, a box = a hotel, it may impose an extra learning task).

Figure 1.3 is taken from a set of materials on the theme of *Au boulot* produced by a Tameside working party.

The least able pupils will benefit from the following approaches:

- taking nothing for granted (e.g. they may not be able to copy easily, to draw or understand a map);
- seeing lots of examples and demonstrations;
- short, simple tasks;
- plenty of space on worksheets to carry out a task;
- effective whole-class teaching, which meets a range of needs and still allows pupils with learning difficulties to blend into the class;
- working in pairs rather than in groups (not all pupils always work well in groups);
- a visual prop or cue which will help when they are listening (word flash cards on the wall, a prompt sheet which the teacher and pupils refer to when the teacher is explaining something);

À la télé...

Replace the pictures with words from the box at the bottom

① Joe Sugden est

② Rod Corkhill est . . . .

③ Mavis est

④ Postman Pat est

⑤ Terry Sullivan est

⑥ Vera Duckworth est

chauffeur
facteur
agent de police
vendeuse
ouvrière
fermier

Figure 1.3

- learning by doing rather than by listening;
- having a range of cues which pupils recognise to serve as shortcuts into memory (e.g. *gestern* or *Dienstag* should be a signal at the start of the lesson for the pupils to volunteer piecemeal the work they covered in the previous lesson).

Be conscious of the pace of your lesson. An able child will become bored if it is too slow; a child with learning difficulties will get lost if things go too quickly and the board is cleared of information before it has been taken in.

There are no glib shortcuts to deal with mixed-ability classes in languages. A differentiated approach can be achieved in many ways, but is rarely easy in any subject, least of all modern languages. Teachers can differentiate by selecting a stimulus which can produce different outcomes, by producing differing stimuli, by varying the learning experience they offer their pupils or by expecting a variety of types of response.

It is possible to meet a wide range of needs with a whole-class teaching approach. Indeed, it is evident that most teachers adopt the whole-class approach for the bulk of the time. However, it is inadvisable to class-teach mixed-ability groups on a permanent basis. Occasionally it is inevitable that different stimuli will be offered to different pupils. Departments or even clusters of departments in a group of schools would be advised to develop banks of differentiated materials to assist in mixed-ability classrooms of all age groups. There will always be a need to break the class down into more manageable teaching groups in order to give different children differentiated tasks. The key to mixed ability may be in the variety of approach.

It is worthwhile engaging in joint ventures with teachers of other subjects in order to tackle work which will benefit each subject (e.g. produce a joint dictionary pack with the English department).

The need for clarity puts in question the whole issue of the use of the target language. Pupils cannot deal with tasks set using the target language unless they are carefully trained to understand, to decipher instructions.

The pupils' perceptions

It is enlightening to take one step backwards to imagine what pupils must perceive in a foreign language lesson. Lessons often involve a lot of repetition. This helps when it gives a pupil time to absorb what is being said or done; it can, however, become counter-productive if pupils find themselves experiencing one of the following:

- the same topics in a different language when they come to learn a second foreign language (e.g. an endless menu of cheese sandwiches) or covering the same material in the same language in different years;
- being set the same task for different topics (for example, asking someone you know well their name, age and address for different reasons, but with the same obvious answers which the questioner could supply without asking the questions each time);

• spending far too long on one topic which is covered in a myriad of ways (for example, asking the way and never really getting anywhere).

Despite the prescriptions of the National Curriculum, the pronouncements of OFSTED and the aspirations of the majority of teachers, the average pupil in a languages classroom in an English school can expect to hear and use a significant amount of English. A realistic approach to the use of the target language is to try to make the most use of it that is appropriate to the group taught. This may be a lot or a little.

Children find language learning stressful; the classroom can be a place of some discomfort. An adult has only to put herself in the same situation with a language alien to her to realise that the activity involves pressure to perform, pressure to 'get it right', little chance to relax, the stress of launching into a sea of the unknown (i.e. the target language). Everything seems to happen quickly in many language lessons. The teacher speeds from activity to activity, with scarcely a pause for breath or wait time, often giving children only limited time to respond to a question or prompt. To this can be added the peer-group pressures already described and the fact that children, unlike adults, do not necessarily choose to study a foreign language.

Pupils are often unaware of what exactly is expected of them and why. They may not see how tasks fit into the general scheme of things, where they are leading and what their point is.

Implications of these pupil perceptions are that different approaches to the same material should be developed. Some courses, particularly at Key Stage 4, could possibly be approached in an unconventional manner, through cross-curricular or assignment-based courses. Chapter 9 gives an example of an assignment-based approach. Where possible, planning should be across the department to avoid unnecessary repetition of material and approach. Instructions and explanations should be repeated in a variety of ways, for example, you can write on the board the same information that you are giving orally. You should consider the gains of giving pupils 'time out' especially in the middle of long or double lessons, or on a Friday afternoon. A concentrated span of pair work or whole-class teaching will be of benefit if it is followed by a few minutes of more relaxed activity, that eases the pressure and offers time for reflection or even a brief chat with a classmate or a teacher. Pupils must, however, be given clear indications of the extent to which this is a privilege and that it will be offered sparingly. It must be stressed to pupils that this privilege is offered on condition that they return to work when you require it.

Invisible children

In every class there are a number of children who go unnoticed: the pupils that James Pye (1989) calls the 'invisible children'. They are not especially clever, especially dull, especially naughty, especially well-behaved. They are just there. They can become so accustomed to being unnoticed that they grow to accept it, even to use it to avoid being involved or doing much work. They usually sit somewhere in the classroom where they know they will not be noticed. This will depend on the teaching habits of individual teachers. Many right-handed teachers concentrate on the right side of the classroom, left-handed teachers on the left; teachers may ignore the pupils directly in front of them and at the front extreme sides. Wherever they sit, invisible pupils are able to be neglected by many teachers. Whole-class teaching could have been invented to create invisible children, as it is well-nigh impossible for a teacher to give every child attention when using a class-teaching approach. Primary school teachers, who get to know their pupils very well, perhaps find it easier to review and reflect on the quality of their interaction with individual pupils. Secondary teachers, reflecting on a week's teaching, may not find it easy to evaluate the quality of their interaction with all their pupils. Has each individual spoken in the target language? Has some aspect of each pupil's work caught the teacher's attention? Are there some pupils who just achieve greater prominence in each lesson? Dealing with this, of course, places increased pressure on the languages teacher to move out of the class-teaching approach wherever possible and appropriate.

Implications for the classroom

- Do an occasional class-scan to check that you have spoken with every child during the previous week. Where 'gaps' appear, deliberately plug them. The longer the gap lasts, the easier it is for invisible children to forget, to unlearn, to ignore the material which the teacher is trying to implant.
- Develop a sense of audience. Watch, listen to the pupils watching, listening to you. You will begin to see the glazed eyes, the distracted look, the quietness which is not simply the quietness which hides an interested mind.
- Set tasks which involve every child in giving you feedback, for example, if you have a small group performing a role-play in front of the class, make sure that all the other groups have a task connected with it, such as assessing expression or accuracy or humour, set by either the teacher or the class. Your drama colleague can give you some useful pointers on criteria, as peer-group assessment is the staple diet of drama lessons.
- Each pupil could have a self-assessment sheet on which she marks various items from time to time.
- Watch out for well-behaved children, particularly the type you usually categorise as 'quiet steady workers'. They can become invisible and be ignored.

Audiences

Pupils have a range of potential audiences for which they can display their foreign language skill. Everyone needs to be appreciated, valued by others. Languages are, after all, a performance subject. The teacher's role includes creating or tapping a variety of audiences for the pupils. These could include:

- other teachers,
- peers,
- younger pupils,
- the whole school,
- e-mail partners in schools overseas,
- parents,
- other adults in the community,
- pen-friends,
- various recipients of letters,
- spectators at public presentations such as fashion shows,
- group discussion lists on the Internet for sixth form students.

Many pupils will happily perform role-plays in front of the teacher as she moves about the classroom and feel important if they receive constructive feedback, be it sincere praise (not a mechanical *Bien!*) or criticism (which shows they are being taken seriously). All feedback must, however, include some praise.

Other teachers who come into the classroom can rapidly be commandeered to become, in a particular activity, a listener, a participant, a victim.

The class teacher can refuse to 'understand' English in a particular lesson, so anyone who enters the room will either have to speak the language being taught or be interpreted by the class, who delight in their superior skills. A visiting foreigner can be used as a target for well-prepared interviews.

Some pupils are natural show-offs and will perform in front of the class. Many, however, dislike it so strongly that they will dread the language lesson because of it. Display of pupils' work, for example on classroom walls, is another way of appealing to an audience or, indeed, to a number of audiences. Pupils can be invited to show, explain, demonstrate their achievement to a neighbour, neighbours or even another class or teacher.

Parents, senior citizens, local employers, other members of the community will be impressed with young people's foreign language skills, if the manner in which they are displayed makes careful allowance for the lack of language skills in the audience.

School events can become a focus for class or year group activities. A parents' evening may involve a French, German, Spanish or Bengali eating place, in which customers are helped to order and are served by using the appropriate language. This could be part of a class assignment (menus, prompts, dialogue practice). Internet searches can provide language resources, even sound files, and background information for such activities.

A cluster of schools, or, if ambition is a sufficiently strong motivator, a single school can organise a *Miniville* or *Kleinstadt* event. This will involve designing language activities to be carried out in a school hall, which becomes for the afternoon a French or German town, with its money exchange, shops, café, post office, souvenir shop, postcards, police and so on. Older pupils can become citizens, while younger pupils, up to a hundred at a time, become tourists. The design and performance of this activity are both ways of providing an audience for spoken and written language. Various departments in a school can combine to make this a cross-curricular venture: modern languages, English, ICT, science, food technology.

In addition to the practical suggestions already made, there are dangers to be recognised. Even the most enthusiastic pupils can become bored with role-plays, if they are the only vehicle for audience involvement. Try jokes, poems, mimes, puppet shows, pupils becoming the teacher to the class, games, posters, corresponding with a class in another school in the town or even further afield, electronic mail projects. Displays of work should recognise the achievement of all pupils, whatever their ability. They can become meaningless if they comprise too many drawings which take pupils a long time to create and include no or very little language. It may be possible to involve other departments in this aspect of your work. You may even give colleagues an idiot's guide to the language you are teaching in order to get them to use the target language in front of the pupils. This is a sensitive issue. Colleagues have their own priorities and many may resent your trying to draw them into your subject. Nevertheless, if only one or two friendly colleagues agree to do this, it is a gain for your language. Teachers can create an audience for the invisible pupils by setting up collaborative group work activities in which everyone can do something. For example, a mini-drama will involve behind-the-scenes work as well as the acting, silent as well as speaking roles.

Chapter 2

Being a teacher

In a work whose main concern is the teaching of modern languages, it may at first seem inappropriate to include a chapter whose focus is general teaching strategies, with less stress on languages than elsewhere in this work. One justification for this is that, as the National Curriculum is gradually slimmed down, the need to review objectives and approaches has not gone away. Indeed, being a teacher means engaging in a continuing evaluation of what and how we teach.

Relationships

Good relationships are at the heart of good classroom practice. Pupils can thrive in an atmosphere of self-respect and respect for others. Being a teacher means, among other things, having antennae which sense audience response.

It is worthwhile asking yourself four questions in this context:

1. *Do you keep up the pressure to work and to be on task, relentlessly?*

Some pupils respond badly to this. That does not mean to say that you must lean too far in the opposite direction and allow slacking. However, it is certainly profitable to build 'time out' into your lesson, as suggested in Chapter 1. It is likely, in a subject such as modern languages teaching, that teachers and their teaching will also benefit from this expedient.

2. *Do your pupils feel comfortable in helping each other?*

Language teachers are often thought to have an obsession with accuracy, with correctness. They may feel constrained by the thought, perhaps misplaced, that they are the main, even the only source of information for pupils to refer to. Inaccuracy can, of course, become a major problem if it interferes with communication or plunges the language user into the wrong register. Learning anything, however, be it a foreign language or a physical skill such as walking, is often based on trial and error. One can learn by trying, having the freedom to make mistakes and trying again in a supportive learning environment, until everything comes right.

It is, therefore, logical that collaborative group and pair work for all four language skills are useful ways of giving individual pupils support. Oral work is the usual activity undertaken in this manner. Reading and writing can equally profit from cooperative work. Pupils often explain matters in a better, more friendly manner than the teacher can adopt, if only in that the teacher is a teacher. Assessment can be undertaken by peers if they are given proper training and support (see Chapter 9). Pupils often ignore and rarely profit from the detailed marking of written exercises which languages teachers see as their lot. Group work on projects can draw on individual pupils' strengths.

The system of 'study buddies' used in some schools merits consideration. If the teacher negotiates with the pairs of pupils concerned, the two or three least able pupils in a class can have named helpers in the same class, who will occasionally go and sit with them to assist. This is productive for both learners.

3. Do you and your pupils get the opportunity to be real people, rather than school people?

If they have a good relationship with the teacher, pupils are often keen to inject some of themselves into the lesson. They may wish to tell you about the latest addition to their family or the summer holiday they spent in a distant country. Almost inevitably the interjection will be in English, even if the class is in full flow on an oral task. This disturbs the flow of the lesson and can be quite disruptive. It may be a deliberate ploy to avoid work on the pupil's part or an unfortunate result of a child's eagerness to share something personal. In either case the teacher should come to an arrangement which will allow pupils' space to be personal and yet avoid disruption. Teachers can negotiate with pupils the most appropriate time for 'news' or 'interruptions'. This could be at the start or at the end of the lesson or during 'time out'.

A sense of humour is essential if a teacher is to remain sane. This is too often reserved for the staffroom, when the most important place in which it should be displayed is in the classroom. It is reasonably easy to inject into the thread of the lesson numerous humorous touches, little asides, light-hearted comments, even jokes. No matter how feeble these humorous elements are, they help to lift the lesson and make it enjoyable for the pupils.

Most teachers care about children, even the most difficult ones. It can do only good if the pupils actually see that the teacher cares about them as individuals, knows their names, knows their nicknames and uses them if it seems right and remembers about their families and friends. A teacher can store large amounts of this kind of information in her head and produce it when appropriate.

It is healthy for pupils to realise that teachers are real people with lives of their own. An important element of the communicative approach is the concentration on the personal, on the here and now, on topics relevant to the learner. This must imply that topics such as booking into a hotel in France, which may well be a part of an examination syllabus or a department's scheme of work, should be balanced against topics which learners may find of more immediate relevance. It makes sense for the teacher to include her or himself in the material being used in the classroom. A good device is to settle the class down at the start of the lesson with a 'running' listening comprehension in the form of a story, which may last two or three minutes each lesson and can draw on the personal experiences of the teacher. A 'running' joke or shaggy dog story can be used in the same way. We have yet to meet the human being who does not like stories. Similar materials can be used for reading work and as a stimulus for the pupils' own written work.

4. *Do your pupils know that you have good days and bad days, just as they do?*

A perfect teacher is not supposed to allow personal matters to affect his or her teaching. It is hard to be perfect! Within reason, it can sometimes be quite in order to tell pupils if you are feeling really well or having an off day, and to expect them to respond accordingly. A good mood may result in a fun lesson, with games and a light atmosphere. A bad mood may mean that you may wish the pupils to 'take it easy on you'. In neither case, of course, would it be appropriate to neglect your pupils. Bad moods should not be frequent (i.e. undisguised on a regular basis). Teaching is partly play-acting, but just occasionally the mask can be allowed to slip. The extent to which this approach can succeed, without being taken advantage of, depends on the relationships which have been built up with the pupils. It must be stressed that this should be a rarely used ploy, for it can soon lose meaning and impact.

Class control

The subject of class control merits a book in itself. This section provides a brief guide. Class control is the aspect of teaching which can make or break a teacher, which can discourage a potential teacher from taking up the profession. Languages teachers can, with some justification, identify additional problems specific to the demands of their subject, caused by the need for pupils to cooperate in the acquisition of skills of which they do not necessarily see the significance and whose acquisition entails a certain amount of 'extrovertness' which teenagers do not always choose to display on demand. This section may run the danger of seeming simplistic, but has a rightful place at a time when there has been a vast increase in the numbers of pupils studying a foreign language at Key Stage 4, which may ease a little as a result of moves to widen options at Key Stage 4 from September 2000.

Maslow (1954, 1970) speaks of a hierarchy of human needs, high among which are the need for the esteem of others and for self-esteem. An approach to class control can be based on this. The way to deal with behavioural problems should be a positive one. Teachers may have recourse, in self-defence, to weapons such as ridicule, humiliation, sarcasm. These may have short-term benefit, but the long-term results vary from brooding resentment to antagonism, from fear to rejection, not counting the damage which is done to the confidence of recipients and the attitude of the rest of the class. One of the authors is tempted to blame his own weakness in German, his first foreign language, on the ridicule which his first German teacher subjected him to for two years. The other suffered similarly in Spanish.

Positive approaches begin with the examination of why pupils misbehave. It may be caused by something beyond your control but not beyond your remedial powers. For example, if the previous lesson has been one in which pupils have been able to run riot or get high in some way, whether because of poor discipline or the nature of the subject being studied, it may be appropriate to start the lesson with a calming activity such as a listening task. If a teacher who taught a class in the previous year was not able to arouse the interest of the class or did not establish a good relationship with it through his own fault, or, equally possibly, theirs, it is important to spend the early weeks creating or re-creating good work habits at the expense of what may be considered valuable course content time. We have both experienced classes which seemed to take a dislike to us for no obvious reason which we could easily identify.

If a previous lesson was one in which the teacher was very strict and kept the pupils under tight rein and the pupils evidently need time to adjust to your style of teaching, the lesson should begin in a manner which prevents the pupils from releasing too much pent up energy without their feeling too repressed.

There are many 'calming' activities which can be used, for example telling the pupils to copy down a list of words you are going to use in the lesson or giving them a dozen words to research for gender, meaning or number in a timed dictionary search.

Children respond better to rewards than to punishments. The persistent misbehaver might misbehave whatever the punishment. Punishment has its place as a last resort and we shall return to this matter soon. By rewarding effort and good behaviour, teachers may be able to encourage their repetition and persistence. Ample opportunities for success must be created. This has implications for the differentiation of tasks where possible. Praise is an important reward. It can take the form of a comment or appreciative smile from the teacher, applause by the class, which can be particularly effective if it spontaneously recognises an effort by someone who rarely makes one. Children like badges. Younger children like to stick or draw a Mr Smiley or a star in their books, if the teacher is pleased with their efforts and authorises it. A fun activity can also be used as a reward, as can 'time out'. Display of work or performance is a type of reward. By putting a pupil's work in a well-presented display you are valuing that work. By asking a pupil to show something or recount something to her neighbour, you are equally giving her the opportunity to feel pride in her achievement.

This leads to the concept of privileges. Wise teachers alert their pupils to the in-class and in-school privileges they have. An in-class privilege is one the pupils gain from being in your classroom. This may be the possibility of doing certain things in your lesson, finishing work five minutes early, having a chat, playing a favourite game and so on. In-school privileges are, for example, having a break, playing games, taking part in a school play, going on a school outing. Removal of any of these privileges can be a useful sanction, though it is unwise to go to extremes in one fell swoop. If you cancel break altogether, pity the poor teacher who receives the pupils after break. On the other hand, additional privileges can be a valid reward. By setting out the possibilities at the start of the term, or the year, the teacher can give pupils something to aim at, either individually or as a class. Of course, if you are aiming at in-school privileges, it is important to check that it is in your power to remove them. For example, it might be worthwhile chatting with the PE teacher before detaining a star player.

If a particular pupil persistently misbehaves, a quiet, frank chat with her or him away from the class may produce the desired effect or at least a respite. Re-seating a pupil can be effective, though it is often wise to move pupils initially in pairs, keeping them with their friends and giving the teacher the chance of one more attempt at control. The teacher can make a 'contract' with such a pupil. This would involve agreeing which behaviours the pupil should try to display and what the teacher would undertake to do in return. The contract can be a detailed one or can set the pupil small targets to aim at initially. For example, the pupil could agree to sit still, to work quietly, to try to control behaviour for five minutes during the next lesson. In return, the teacher could agree to try to ignore the less flagrant misbehaviours in that lesson. Thereafter, the contract can be discussed, reviewed and re-negotiated regularly. This may seem simplistic and must be handled carefully, lest the pupil concerned should think that he or she is 'special' or receiving favourable treatment because of being difficult. Wherever possible, confrontations should be avoided. The teacher will rarely 'win' in that situation. A word with the pupil away from the class, deprives her or him of part of the aim behind the misbehaviour: an audience and attention.

If the whole class is disruptive, a change of activity can be effective. There is no point in continuing with an activity, no matter how well-prepared, if it is not working. When all possible approaches to class or pupil control have been tried and failed, teachers may resort to punishments. If you start small and gradually build up, you can leave yourself with something in reserve. So, five minutes of something highly controlled, for example structured writing, can be one step in a gradually increasing hierarchy of punishments. Threats and promises must be kept. Pupils soon spot weaknesses, if you are prone to break either of these.

Implications for the classroom

It must be stressed that what works for one teacher may not work for another. Points made below refer to classes which contain potential behaviour problems, but are also applicable to all classes, for all classes can potentially misbehave.

- Set tasks which suit the class. A class of fifteen-year-olds of average or just below average ability, some of whom are disruptive, will not take kindly to being asked to absorb and learn tracts of abstract grammar or to read aloud (or worse, to listen to one pupil reading aloud) a stretch of prose in a foreign language which means little or nothing to them.
- The importance of understanding cannot be over-emphasised. A class of pupils who have lost entirely the meaning of what is going on will become restless. Checks on understanding can include a recap, a quick couple of questions, a class-scan to see if there are signs of pupils getting lost. It is useful

to introduce the odd word or words in English to explain if there has been a sustained period of target language use by the teacher which may mean little or nothing to some of them. See Chapter 6 for a more detailed discussion of the use of English.

- Contrary to received opinion, many pupils may not necessarily benefit from overlong bouts in the target language. Here again, the importance of understanding is significant. Simple exposure is not enough, the language needs to be mediated, made comprehensible and accessible, so that it can be gradually acquired.
- The correction of 'errors' can stimulate resentment and bad behaviour if it is handled insensitively. A pupil who knows that each time she opens her mouth to say something in the target language, she will be pounced upon by the teacher eager to help the pupil achieve perfection, will be prone to resent it and react accordingly, either by misbehaving or shutting off.
- Set practical rather than abstract tasks, doing things rather than listening to a lot of teacher talk, or reading a written text which lacks stimulation encourage concentration and commitment. Compare:

(a) Working in pairs to produce an e-mail which will be sent to another pair or an agreed destination later in the lesson, after the teacher has discussed a few examples and given pairs a chance to improve their originals;
(b) The class silently read a passage in German about the coast of North Germany and then answer literal questions orally in English.

- Break the class into small teaching groups when possible. Pairs may be more manageable than groups with some classes. If you are blessed with an FLA, use her with difficult classes in particular as a teaching partner.
- To punish pupils rather than apply a positive approach to behaviour management is tantamount to an admission of defeat, but there will always be situations for all teachers where every other alternative has failed.

The hierarchy of punishments can be broken down into very small gradations. For example:

(a) In your control:

- a smile;
- a brief stare (though care is needed not to be confrontational);
- a warning;
- a raised eyebrow;
- a frown;
- a quick word which others do not hear (if possible);
- a more prolonged comment which other pupils do not hear;
- a chat at the end of the lesson warning of future action;
- withdrawal of a privilege;
- detaining for part of break;
- detention after school;
- report to someone else.

(b) Outside your control:

• involve the Senior Management Team;
• involve parents.

Body language

There are many signals sent by the teacher which are not directly connected with the meaning of the words they utter in the classroom. Body language and other overlays, which are not strictly speaking verbal ones, contribute considerably to the atmosphere of a lesson. They can also add to the meaning of what the teacher is trying to convey.

Smiles and nods are visible signs of approval and encouragement. They help to create a relaxed atmosphere conducive to work. The lack of these can create an over-serious, intense atmosphere which can increase classroom tensions.

Facial expression conveys a wealth of messages, from sincerity to wrath. Of course, the teacher is an actor, among other things, and has to be able to control the expressions he wishes to use. The eyebrows tell the main story to those who have been taught or have learnt to read them. Your gaze can be used to imply approval, attention, warning, anger.

Tone of voice underlines meaning. A teacher can use loudness and softness of voice as a teaching aid. It is easy to accustom a class to habitual shouting, so that, when you really want to attract its attention, your shouting has no impact. A quiet voice demands attention; pupils have to strain to hear it and, so long as it is saying something interesting or important, they will be quiet in order to pick up the message. The occasional raised voice can be very effective.

The positioning of the teacher is an interesting issue. Sitting behind a desk is a well-protected position but it does not allow the teacher to reach trouble spots quickly to nip problems in the bud, nor does it encourage a relaxed relationship between pupils and the teacher. Sitting on the desk is quite different. There is no barrier and the teacher appears informal and relaxed. Teachers should, however, be prepared to move about the classroom, whether the mode used is class-teaching, pair or group work.

Crouching next to pupils as you visit the different groups, pairs or individuals is warmer and less threatening, less condescending than looming over them. Crouching is friendly, relaxed, and informal.

Gesture, facial expression and mime support meaning. A lot of communication is non-verbal. Indeed, as much as 90 per cent of communication is non-verbal. The teacher can use eyebrows, the whole face, hands, a pointing finger and the rest of the body to make quite clear to pupils what is meant by words in the target language they are dealing with. The whole body is part of the teacher's repertoire of teaching materials. Some teachers are 'natural'; many, however, need to develop an awareness of the power of their own bodily expressions and to use them consciously once they realise how that skill works. In this way difficult language can be made comprehensible. The great danger in this is that the pupils can easily come to rely on these supports for meaning and will not even listen to the words uttered. In order to avoid this, teachers should consciously develop a policy of gradually diminishing support. Little by little those gestures and expressions which provide an alternative for the actual words and act as support strategies (Johnstone 1989) would be withdrawn, forcing the pupils to listen and/or read. This means, for example, that the teacher will have to resist the temptation to point to objects every time they are mentioned.

Yes, it all sounds very self-conscious and artificial, even hypocritical. Teaching is an art which only a minority practise with flair; the rest of us common mortals have to work at it!

Classroom organisation

Children enjoy variety and delight in the unexpected, so long as it does not damage them. Growing up is, after all, an adventure. When lessons become so set in their format that the pupil can switch off and go into automatic pilot, knowing she will not be noticed, there is a danger, even a likelihood that learning will not really take place. Variety in classroom organisation should at least be part of the teacher's arsenal of approaches. Many teachers use a variety of organisational ploys to create a lively atmosphere conducive to work. The choice of classroom organisation will be influenced by many factors, for example:

- the number of pupils in the class;
- the size and ability of the class;
- the aim of the lesson;
- the size and shape of the room and whether it has desks or tables;
- the mood of the class;
- the availability of a carpet;
- the time of day;
- what happened in the previous lesson;
- the availability of technology.

Whatever style you adopt, there must be ground rules between you and your classes. It may be wise to set them at the start of the year and to remind pupils of them every now and then. Ground rules can draw on all or any of the following:

- use of the target language;
- noise levels;
- respect for each other;
- listening to each other;
- agreeing when to stop and how;
- length of time for an activity;
- privileges;
- monitoring each other for behaviour, contribution to a task, being on task, using English;
- monitoring the teacher's use of English;
- keeping promises;

- participating may be optional for certain agreed activities;
- avoiding hurting each other.

Whole-class teaching

Whole-class teaching is the traditional approach to working with pupils and has a crucial role in the repertoire of teaching approaches. It is undoubtedly the preferred teaching mode of many teachers. The number of children this method of organisation forces the teacher to deal with has a number of advantages and disadvantages.

The main advantages are:

1. It is an effective way of:

    - transferring information,
    - demonstrating new ideas,
    - target-setting and reviewing,
    - explaining grammar,
    - setting up a new activity,
    - modelling an activity,
    - giving instructions,
    - doing background work,
    - organising general listening activities,
    - listening to a story,
    - brainstorming for a letter or a piece of writing,
    - setting up a role-play or brainstorming vocabulary.

2. Standing in front of the class, the teacher can use observational skills to engage and monitor the pupils, moving the focus of response and involvement about the classroom.
3. It is the least stressful for the teacher to organise and, from some points of view, the easiest.
4. The chalk board, whiteboard, electronic whiteboard, overhead projector or cassette recorder can draw the pupils' eyes and ears to the front of the room and encourage concentration.
5. The teacher can easily do a class scan to monitor the class and pick out potential problems.

The main disadvantages are:

1. It is not always an economical use of teacher or pupil time. The teacher cannot deal with a large number of pupils at one and the same time. Whole-class teaching is not necessary even for writing and listening work.
2. Children can easily hide in the whole-class environment, even become invisible, leading children to believe or hope that the teacher never bothers with them.
3. Children become bored waiting for their turn to speak in an oral lesson, especially if the pace is allowed to drop.

Because of the nature of whole-class teaching, it takes great skill to overcome the disadvantages when they predominate. If the teacher is prepared to move about the classroom during a whole-class lesson, it will help. Modern linguists claim that the nature of their subject requires a high proportion of class teaching. If this were the case, it would substantiate the case against mixed-ability teaching in modern foreign languages, when it is difficult to teach the class as a single group for a sustained period of time. It is, however, possible to devise methods of enabling the pupil to become independent, thus freeing the teacher to make a more economical use of energy.

Variants on whole-class teaching

Pupils can take over the role of the teacher for the whole or part of the lesson. This is a novelty which releases the teacher and develops communication skills in pupils. Its uses are limited to the following types of task:

● presentation from a group activity;
● modelling or leading an activity for the class;
● role-playing the teacher.

The class can sit or stand in a circle or form two circles facing each other. This gives a lot more eye contact and makes it easier for the pupils to concentrate on and listen to each other. It does take time to set up. It can be used for:

● making a pupil the leader of an activity in the centre of a circle;
● games such as number games or 'add an item' games;
● preparing a topic;
● telling a story;
● preparing for a speaking test;
● rapid variation in partner work, by linking pupils in different parts of the circle, two at a time;
   – discussion of progress of the class's work;
   – a vocabulary brainstorm;
   – thanks, congratulations, applause.

Group and pair work

Group work has been the oft-preached ideal for many years. It has its advantages and dangers.

Advantages of group work

● It has attractive socialising effects, facilitating collaborative and cooperative working, teamwork.
● It makes learning relaxed and enjoyable.
● Many minds can be more productive than one.
● Group work encourages ownership and involvement.

- It allows the less able child to get unobtrusive support and able children can be stimulated by the opportunity to explain, to contribute, to teach.
- Simulations and practical activities can take place; pupils can make things and board games can be played.
- Pupils become more responsible for their own behaviour.
- Written tasks can be marked.
- Background information can be researched.

Dangers of group work and how to avoid them

A teacher's normal class control strategies will not work and noise levels will increase. Each teacher must have her own signal to shut down group activity immediately if the noise level becomes too high. It can be a clapping of hands or a particular word said loudly. The teacher must be more tolerant of noise than is her wont. Make a 'contract' with the class on teamship, noise levels, being on task. Neighbouring teachers should be warned and an agreement of what they can tolerate arrived at.

Pupils quickly lose their work momentum and start chatting or doing something other than what the teacher intends. They have to be taught how to work in groups. They will learn to monitor each other's contributions to the group task and will often become a more efficient control mechanism than the teacher! Nevertheless the teacher may have to accept that the attitude to work will be much more relaxed. There will still be much more practice achieved than is possible when the teacher is class teaching.

It can be very time-consuming to create group tasks which are self-regulatory. Much depends on the aim of the lesson. The teacher may wish all the groups to undertake the same task. This is definitely an economical way of using material. It is just as economical to create a carousel of tasks, which each group will undertake during a lesson or series of lessons. Differentiated work to suit the needs of different abilities certainly takes time to create and is best done as part of a department's strategy to produce materials for their materials bank, with each member of the department taking on part of the workload.

There is certainly a potential for behaviour problems. Much depends upon the class's ability to cope with the demands. Make it a privilege to work in groups. Key Stage 3 pupils in many instances are easier to manage in pairs than in groups. Key Stage 4 pupils, hopefully more mature, often respond more positively to group work.

Group work is difficult but very worthwhile and pair work is also a useful method of developing cooperative learning. It has many of the attractions of group work and has the added attraction of leaving the teacher more in control of classroom events. It is particularly appropriate for teachers who lack the confidence or class control to become involved in group work techniques. With new classes it is a profitable way forward until the teacher is accustomed to the pupils and the pupils are accustomed to the teacher. Set up quickly, it is the ideal way of approaching oral activities. There are many examples of pair activities in later chapters.

Variants on group work

The 'goldfish bowl' technique adds to the group a pupil observer. This can be used for assessment of group work or simple feedback. The observer can be given criteria to use in the assessment (e.g. presentation, quality of language, team skills, initiative). It can be used for a simulation in which a number of people get in and out of a lift. As people get in or out they chat with each other. The observer's task is to note all the information she gleans as she stays in the lift for the whole journey as a 'fly on the wall' radio commentator. This can be adapted to suit a doctor's waiting room, a corner shop, a local train, a family meal in which the participants have been briefed that certain things must happen during the course of the meal, such as the arrival of a long-lost relative.

The carousel arrangement permits an integrated classroom organisation. It allows the teacher to run a variety of activities at the same time, which the pupils can visit either in the order they choose or under the teacher's direction. In the same room, six children can work at a listening centre, carrying out a listening task, while another four collaborate in a writing activity around a word processor or simply at a table with pen and paper, another six practise oral work, while another six will be finding out background information. The rest of the class can be undertaking individual tasks or some of the tasks already mentioned. The teacher will be moving about the classroom to give support where needed, though the collaborative approach which has been established will release the teacher to concentrate her efforts at chosen spots. This takes a lot of planning, but can be a time saver in the long run, as the tasks repeat themselves over a lengthy period until all groups have carried out those tasks which are appropriate.

At the start of the new millennium, the use of ICT in modern language lessons is still not well advanced. By 2002, this situation will have altered quite radically. Teachers are already coming to terms with the possibilities of ICT and schools are rapidly gearing up to provide access to the whole curriculum. Initiatives such as the National Grid for Learning and New Opportunities Funding are offering access to ICT for all teachers and providing training and hardware to facilitate the computer confidence and competence these policies promise. As the twenty-first century dawns, this teaching aid will increasingly be part of the language teacher's repertoire. Chapter 11 deals with this topic.

The computer can be used for group and, more easily, pair work. If more than one pupil sits at a terminal, it is essential that the teacher has trained them to allocate and vary roles, so that there are no disputes and each pupil is actively involved.

Team teaching

A team can comprise the class teacher and any of the following: an FLA, another colleague (whether a fellow linguist or one from another part of the curriculum), an ICT coordinator, a special needs support teacher or classroom assistant, an older pupil. Team teaching has disadvantages:

- it is threatening to the class teacher;
- it has timetabling implications;
- it can make demands on the size of a teaching area.

On the other hand, its advantages are attractive:

- It shares the workload of organisation, preparation and class control.
- It extends the choice of activity and puts pupils in contact with more adults.
- If classes are combined, it puts pupils in contact with new work partners.

Activities include:

- cross-curricular work at Key Stage 4 (food technology, for example, making dishes);
- teachers working in two separate rooms but planning and working as a team;
- asking another class to assess written work or oral work done by your own class.

Special needs support can be used in a variety of ways. Support teachers can sit alongside pupils with learning difficulties to give them a hand. Much better is to team-teach with them, so that no child is singled out as different. They can also help you design appropriate materials and plan lessons. ESL support often takes the form of collaborative teaching across the curriculum, in which English is learnt through the intermediary of the subject being taught. This could provide a model for the teaching of a foreign language.

Classes move about

Several activities can be organised with the members of a class moving about the room, usually to undertake oral work of some kind and provide pupils with new speaking partners. Such movement can energise pupils and give them a feeling of independence. Of course, the obvious danger is noise, leading to chaos. This will draw on class control skills. Activities in this mode include:

- Who, what am I? (give pupils a name, a job, a word, an object, an animal pinned to their back and they have to find out by asking questions as they move about);
- Find your partner (give out pairs of names, objects, rubrics for the GCSE; pupils ask questions or 'chat' to find their partner);
- Find someone who ... (has three sisters, a dog, lives in Blackpool, has been to Paris, etc.).

The instructions for these activities can be in target language or English, according to the level of ability of the class.

Variations on moving about

Lines of pupils facing each other down the classroom or even in the corridor outside can be given oral tasks such as conducting surveys or speaking about themselves in ever-increasing detail. After each turn, the person at one end of a line on the left moves to the end of the line and the rest move up a place. Then, after a further oral interaction, this is repeated and so on.

Going out of the room or the building

Pupils can be allowed to leave the room for some activities. They can go to the library for research or to prepare an activity. They can venture much further. On specially organised occasions, visits can be organised to a local café or place connected with the target language which can be staffed with native speakers. Older pupils can also be sent to work with younger ones, to read their own stories to them or support them. Intensive language mornings in the school hall, a miniature languages festival or simulated French town or German railway station will all spark excitement for languages. Cross-school links or links between classes also move pupils away from the usual environment. The ultimate way out of the classroom (though without the pupils leaving it) is via the Internet and learners can be asked to acquire information from target language sources.

Flexible learning

Though flexible learning is a distinct possibility, few language teachers use it in their lessons. One method of introducing flexible learning is to place all the resources at a teacher's disposal, including human resources, such as the FLA and the teacher himself, at the disposal of the class. Tasks are set, with tight deadlines and according to a contract negotiated with the class, groups or individuals. The pupils then set about the tasks. The work becomes self-monitoring and releases the teacher to offer support where it is most needed. For instance, a Year 10 class or groups within it can be given the task of finding out all they can about the main events of interest in a given week in Germany. They can use newspapers, a radio with headphones, the teacher, magazines, the World Wide Web, the library and other sources. The contract negotiated may include the insistence on the use of German or use of German sources. This leads to each group presenting its results in a different format: a bulletin, a chart, a news broadcast, a web page. The teacher will have to ensure that each member of each group has agreed tasks, deadlines, participation. This is, of course, not the only way of approaching flexible learning.

Conclusion

No single form of classroom organisation is sufficient in itself for the delivery of any subject or, indeed, for a single lesson. Teachers who draw on the full range of possibilities can enliven their teaching at will.

The arrangement of the classroom influences the range of the possibilities. If you wish on occasion to use techniques other than whole-class teaching, it is worth experimenting with classroom arrangements other than the traditional rows of desks or tables. Tables may be arranged in groups of two or four joined together for group or pair work as well as whole-class teaching. Desks or tables may be arranged in a horseshoe formation around the walls of the room to facilitate circle and line work. It is quite easy to get the class to face the teacher at those times when the attention of the whole class is needed. Much of lesson time can be spent with pupils not facing the front. However, just as whole-class teaching is the preferred mode of many teachers, classrooms arranged in serried rows of tables are also the preferred arrangement of many teachers. If this is what they prefer and it still produces the range of language learning activity described in this chapter, no one can criticise them.

The last words in this section must be cautionary. Whole-class teaching may be your frequent delivery style. By using other approaches, you will enliven your teaching and reach pupils that other styles seldom reach. You will be able to provide more opportunities for practice, learning and understanding the language. Any change of approach must, however, be carefully planned and gently introduced. Change can be exciting, but it can also be unsettling. Our advice is that you should always try out anything new in the best possible conditions, in other words, with a class that will present the least 'challenge'. Once you have ironed out the creases, you can use it with more demanding classes.

Section 2: Teaching and learning in the foreign language classroom

Chapter 3

Stages in foreign language teaching

Recent practice has been dominated by communicative approaches which put the emphasis on communication, seeking to engage learners in genuine use of the language in authentic situations. It is probably fair to say that applications of these approaches (despite many disputes about the identity of communicative methods!) have led to greater enjoyment and motivation. Communicative approaches have offered ways forward in language teaching, though we do not wish to suggest that all classroom exercises and activities can and must be communicative. For this reason, we prefer to consider the task as being one of teaching for communicative purposes. If methods help learners to acquire language successfully so that they can go on to communicate, then they are valid. The successful language teacher does not confine herself to one method, to the exclusion of others (Richardson 1983, p. 19). In this chapter we consider the most common features of language teaching practised in many schools today. GCSE courses and examinations give equal weight to all four skills (LSRW), though some learners may opt out of some tiers of assessment, for example, a higher level writing paper. The key objective at Key Stages 3 and 4 is communicating in the target language. This remains the case at sixth form level, though other dimensions such as culture and explicit knowledge about the language acquire greater importance.

Communication and communicative competence

We acknowledge that communicative competence is seen as the aim, an appropriate ambition for language learning. By this is understood the ability to adapt to different contexts and use language to receive and send appropriate messages. This is very different to the artificial non-communicative manipulation of language, so characteristic of grammar–translation methods. However, we do not insist that foreign language competence equates with native speaker competence.

For practical purposes, we can say that people are motivated to communicate when they have a reason for so doing. They are readily able to send and receive messages when they have the language to do so and a clear purpose. The communication may involve interaction either socially or functionally (for example in a bank). It could also mean using a range of resources, not just face-to-face encounters: telephone, fax, e-mail, possibly even video-conferencing. Such considerations now have a significant bearing on the conduct of language teaching.

How effectively can we develop foreign language communication in the standard classroom? When 'communicative methods' are badly applied, learners are exposed to the unvaried practice of a succession of transactions often in the form of tightly controlled role-plays. Well-managed approaches draw on strategies, traditional and new, to create a lively, interactive classroom where language is learnt, used and enjoyed in a variety of ways. Naturally, we want to move in this direction but it should not be to the exclusion of all other considerations, for example the possible value of traditional methods in meeting learner needs.

Communicative approaches have their limitations. After all, language learning takes place in a classroom, a deliberately constructed setting, not a genuine open environment for 'natural' communication and language acquisition. Learning a language is not the same as using a language (Swan 1985). The classroom is often far removed from the reality of the target language community. Attempts to bridge this gap will, we suggest, assist language learning but we do not have to be 'authentic' for the sake of it. There are increasing opportunities for use of language in real communicative settings through the Internet and it is right that teachers are trained to take advantage of these opportunities for meaningful interaction. However, we should not lose sight of the limits within which any approach or method is applied.

Appropriate teaching styles

Traditional up-front whole-class teaching has an important role to play in the transmission of new language, in orchestrating practice, in clarifying language patterns. It can give inspiration, purpose and direction to learners. It is a vital part of the language teacher's repertoire but on its own rarely provides for enough interaction between pupils. Opportunities for questioning, opinion-seeking, offering ideas and suggestions, initiating conversation – such features incorporated into lessons help to establish a productive balance between transmission and interaction. Through transmission methods the teacher may build up the store of language to which learners have access; interaction allows learners the opportunities to fulfil a communicative purpose and make that knowledge more automatic. Success in communicating is believed to increase the level of communicative competence. So, the design of activities should take into account:

(a) the desire to communicate
(b) the purpose
(c) the language needed
(d) the likely degree of success that learners will enjoy.

When these factors exist in an encouraging and lively atmosphere, learners are more likely to be engaged and there is a greater likelihood of success and enjoyment. A traditional model of language teaching is sometimes called P-P-P, because it has three stages: presentation, practice, production (Littlewood 1981) or presentation, practice, use (Atkinson and Lazarus 1997, p. 2). For the sake of simplicity, we refer to them as:

1. The presentation stage: getting the language in.
2. The practice stage: keeping it there.
3. The communication stage: getting the language out.

New language is introduced, then practised in pre-communicative activities, before the learners make freer use of it in role-play, unpredictable situations, assignments and even spontaneous outbursts! It is most easily understood in relation to the productive skills of speaking and writing, but communication and communicative competence apply equally to reading and listening.

Here, we have a workable framework on which to hang the demands of the job but it is not given as a perfect model. The stages merge into one another and distinctions, for example between advanced practice stages and communication, often blur. To the stages listed, revision or re-cycling should be added as Stage 4. Revision may occur when an initial introduction fails to offer a guiding model to learners, while a presentation may be a re-cycling of old language. Inadequate performance by pupils at the communication stage suggests the need for revision.

What do we mean by each of the stages: presentation, practice and communication? What should they look like?

1. The presentation stage

(a) Introducing new language

For new language, the manner of presentation varies with resources available, for example:

- teacher alone as model
- teacher with assistant(s) (where employed!)
- teacher and pupil modelling language
- teacher and chalkboard/whiteboard
- teacher and overhead projector
- listening to or reading a text
- self-access materials (worksheets, tapes, CD-ROMS, Web pages, books).

At this hearing or seeing stage, the priority is to provide clear, accurate models that learners will have the opportunity to examine, imitate and use, i.e. appropriate comprehensible input, to borrow a phrase from Krashen (1985), though perhaps not in the way he would prefer. The teacher, if involved, presents meaning and form, while checking comprehension and generating enthusiasm. This is a tightly controlled stage of the process during which learners are corrected, but in a supportive, non-menacing way.

(b) Re-cycling 'old' language

The presentation may be a review or recall of something already taught, perhaps shown in a new way or context. Many lessons follow such a pattern, typically beginning with an elicitation exercise that draws the language from assorted learners. A teacher and pupil modelling language is not uncommon in recycling or revision phases. This also has the benefit of involving learners in contributing models of language and valuing them as a reliable resource.

2. The practice stage

Ideally, a clear, motivating presentation is followed by the maximum possible amount of practice by learners. It is widely believed that the more practice is organised for students the more their familiarity and confidence grow. During this stage, the teacher prompts utterances and offers guidance. This stage is sometimes divided into:

• controlled practice;
• guided practice.

Controlled-practice activities seek a near-perfect rendering of the language presented and the teacher monitors and corrects. Sufficient practice is given to allow learners to get it right. Perhaps the simplest form of controlled practice is repetition – learning by saying what a teacher or tape has said, for example.

During guided practice, teacher control or support relaxes as activities begin to move towards the communicative end of the spectrum by offering greater opportunities for learning by doing. The emphasis begins to change from getting the form right to getting a message across. In a sense, the teacher is encouraging pupils to take risks with language, albeit in a safe, supportive environment. The teacher ideally monitors and considers where to go next – revision or communication. Monitoring does not mean close supervision. If the teacher is too intrusive or over-corrects, the pupil could be deterred from trying things out for fear of correction.

3. The communication stage

This is the stage when our learners engage in meaningful, interactive tasks where success depends on the presence of a purpose and a need to communicate. This is the stage when learners are activated (Harmer 1998) so that they use the fruits of their study in using the language. The emphasis is on the receipt and transmission of message, on effective communication occurring despite occasional imperfections of form. The degree of encouragement for risk-taking is greater at this stage. If language learning involves experimentation and risk-taking, errors are seen as formative, part of the process of exploring language independently, coping with the unpredictable and discovering new information. During oral work, unless communication breaks down, teacher interference should be minimal. With written work, a similar approach can be applied so that learners are guided not just on their accuracy but also on the way they manage to communicate through writing.

The key is to take the fear out of speaking and writing in the foreign language. Learning a language has authenticity and purpose and, as noted above at the practice stage, intervening in a continual way to correct errors could be counter-productive for many learners. A balance needs to be struck between teacher guidance and allowing opportunities for formative communicative activity.

Gradually diminishing support

From presentation through to communication the principle of gradually diminishing support (GDS) operates. The teaching style can move from transmission to organisation of practice to facilitation of communication. In the early stages lots of gesture, mime and other visual support may be offered. In addition to guidance from the teacher, other forms of support include students helping one another, translation of key vocabulary, support from computer programs and traditional materials such as books and worksheets. As learners become more confident and their language grows, so the amount of support should be reduced. They should be forewarned that support will be gradually removed and that they will be expected to become more and more independent.

During communicative activities the support is sharply reduced. If the reduction is premature the communication may not succeed and the teacher may decide to return the group or class to a practice drill. If practice activities run into serious difficulty learners may require the support of another presentation

STAGE	TEACHING STYLE	LEARNING STYLE	INTERACTION
Presentation	Transmission	Reception	Teacher/class
			Teacher/group
			Teacher/student
			Material/class
Practice	Organisation	Manipulation	Teacher/class
		G	Teacher/student
		D	Pairs
		S	Groups
			Teacher/student
Communication	Facilitation	Production	Pairs, Groups; Creative interaction; books; native speakers and databases etc.
		Independent use of language	

Figure 3.1

(probably a different one) or some other type of support, such as repetition of important phrases, reminders about the way to structure a piece of writing, for example, a letter to a public office.

Communicative competence does not result from a flat, featureless stroll but rather a spiral of steps, leaps and perhaps even some falls. However, Figure 3.1 attempts a summary of the major transitions that occur on the winding way.

The information or opinion gap

The desire to communicate is governed by the need to give or acquire information. Where there is no need, it is difficult to see how there can be 'real communication'. The use of flashcards in the classroom may illustrate this point. A teacher can ask students to tell them what is on the picture. The information is known to everyone. The response may be a model of correct usage but there is no exchange of information.

This is a common and useful drill but everyone can see the information transmitted. This type of cued response practises the language but it does not communicate any new message. On the other hand, students may be asked to engage in a guessing game to find out what the weather is like in certain places:

Che tempo fa?

Figure 3.2

The teacher reverses the cards and asks students:

Che tempo fa a Roma? a Napoli? a Berlino?

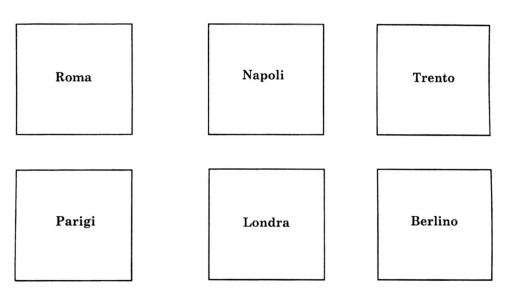

Figure 3.3

Pupils offer responses from their language store, for example:

Fa caldo; fa freddo; piove,

with the guesses continuing until someone gives the correct answer and wins the card.

So, we have a simple information gap. The teacher has the information but the learner does not know and may be motivated to guess in order to find out. Similarly, if we seek opinions from people, not knowing how they will answer, we have an opinion gap. So, it is likely that one learner will know how a friend will answer when asked:

Que penses-tu des professeurs?

but have less of an idea when asking:

Que penses-tu de ce groupe?
Que penses-tu de ce programme?

in relation to a video or audio presentation, just viewed.

If pupils always know the 'answers' there is no need for thought, speculation or listening or reading for meaning. Information gaps generate enthusiasm and opportunities for 'real' use of pupils' existing language. More complicated information gaps can be set, suitable for Key Stage 4 and sixth form classes:

Tu as gagné un concours vacances. Une agence de voyage t'offre le choix de cinq destinations au mois d'octobre. Tu dois t'informer au sujet des cinq destinations pour faire un choix raisonnable. Tu aimes le beau temps, la mer, les petites villes. Tu n'aimes pas la circulation, les températures extrêmes et les discos. Pose des questions à l'agent de voyage et remplis les cases.

Voyageur

Ville	Climat	Température moyenne en octobre	Pays et Région
Ajaccio			
Nice			
Oran			
Cayenne			
Dakar			

Figure 3.4

Agent de voyage

Ville	Climat	Température moyenne en octobre	Pays et Région
Ajaccio	doux, beau, averses	20C	Capitale de la Corse, île dans la Méditerranée
Nice	doux, beau	19C	Grande ville de la Côte d'Azur Sud de la France. Riche
Oran	chaud, soleil	28C	Grand port de l'Algérie en Afrique du Nord. Plage polluée
Cayenne	humide, chaud, pluvieux	32C	Guinée en Amérique du sud. Plage
Dakar	chaud, soleil	34C	Capitale du Sénégal et centre de tourisme

Figure 3.5

In order to make an informed choice the student playing the part of the traveller needs to find out what the weather and temperature are for the different places, thus bridging an information gap. Follow-up activities are possible:

• practice of comparatives in speech/writing;

- writing reasons for wanting to visit one place;
- writing reasons for not wishing to visit the other places;
- explaining one's choice orally to the group or class;
- small groups go to the library or ICT room to do more research on the places and write a profile of each.

Accuracy and error

At the presentation and early practice stages of speaking and writing activities, getting the language right is the key purpose, that is to say, correct pronunciation, spelling, usage. Learners are required to concentrate on form.

The Modern Foreign Languages for Ages 11–16 proposals (DES 1990) stated: 'we think it important to recognise that in fact pupils often learn through making mistakes, and that they should not be discouraged from experimenting with the language.'

The 1990 document has of course been superseded but it contains much sound advice. Attention is also drawn to the fact that language learning is an uneven process – not a horizontal, linear, smoothly progressive development. Such beliefs lead us to conclude that genuine attempts at communication should be welcomed and praised. We believe that such considerations remain valid however many times a curriculum might be revised, the curriculum for 2000 included.

Carefully planned lessons allow for error correction, confirmation of good work and revision where appropriate. If growing competence depends on opportunities to perform within a motivating and supportive framework, constant correction of errors will probably demotivate large numbers of learners.

The time and place for error correction is a feature that can be profitably discussed and negotiated even with young learners. When they recognise that some parts of the lesson involve error correction while periods of communication allow interruption-free performance, they may perceive more of the purpose of what they are about in the language classroom without red-faced embarrassment or red ink. A range of techniques can be used to focus on error in a formative way:

- summing up errors seen or heard, at the end of an activity without identifying any pupil;
- in written work, underlining a single sentence in four or five students' writing, these are then written on the board to create a short text and students in small groups are asked to consider how they can be improved;
- issuing remedial guidance (for example, an item of vocabulary, a model sentence, an example of the structure to use) to individuals or groups on cards or pieces of paper when they are engaged in a group or writing task.

Error correction is further considered in Chapter 6.

The language skills (LSRW)

Communicative competence depends on a balanced development of four language skills: understanding when listening (L), making oneself understood when speaking (S), understanding meaning when reading (R) (not just reading to learn the language), and writing with purpose (W). In practical terms, a series of well-planned lessons assures a balanced and integrated package of skills development. Separation of the skills for public examination and profiling purposes does not mean that lessons should be parcelled in that way. Lessons may have a particular focus on one or two skills, or the four skills may be integrated. Oral work in the form of formative talk should be a feature of all lessons (reading and discussing; generating ideas for writing; responding to spoken texts, etc.). In the past, there may also have been a view that language lessons should follow the LSRW order. The result could often be that writing was relegated to the end of lesson, largely devoted to copying downs models of language. However, lessons can and often do begin with reading or speaking or writing.

The skills fit into the process of language learning on the principle of gradually diminishing support. Here are some examples to illustrate what kind of activities a 14–16-year-old might experience at different stages of learning in secondary school foreign language lessons which follow a presentation–practice–communication model:

Topic: Leisure, free time and entertainment

1. Listening

- Presentation: Hearing single words, short phrases, dialogues perhaps supported by flashcards or worksheets, short texts.
- Practice:

  - Predicting what they are about to hear.
  - Listening and repeating words or phrases.
  - Listening and identifying main points in the text.
  - Listening and ticking boxes.

- Communication: More able students may listen to and understand: announcements, conversation, music, a video-film (Pagnol's *La Gloire de Mon Père* at Year 12–13 level), satellite TV snippets.

2. Speaking

- Presentation: For less able students, the teacher mimes the actions and presents vocabulary and phrases, for example, *il danse, il tricote, il nage,* or past-time equivalents, depending on the stage of learning.
- Practice:

  - Repetition of phrases and vocabulary.
  - Responding to flashcards.
  - Responding to teacher questions (all abilities, as the questions can be graded to suit learners, abilities and interests).
  - Pair work with cue cards.
  - Survey/questionnaire on hobbies (can cater for a range of abilities).

- Communication: Talking freely about one's leisure, for example, to the assistant(e), to peers, visitors.

3. Reading

- Presentation: Single written words, phrases on card, text related to hobbies for example, letter, brochure.
- Practice:

    - Reading for recognition for example, free time words like *la natation, le cheval.*
    - Reading and matching for example, hobbies to people.
    - Reading for general understanding and making notes.
    - Predicting the content of a text before reading to see how far they are correct.

- Communication:
    - Reading a letter.
    - Reading journal articles to find out about entertainment enjoyed by young people in the target language (sixth form).
    - Reading a story for pleasure (reading material is available for all levels).

4. Writing

- Presentation: Viewing the printed word, then copying (early stages of learning).
- Practice:

    - Tracing over new items of language.
    - Matching words/phrases to pictures.
    - Copying selected phrases.
    - Filling in gaps.
    - Ordering a jumbled narrative.
    - Completion of phrases.
    - Finishing texts.
    - Imitating other texts.
    - Having 'fun with texts' on a word processor.

- Communication:

    - Writing a letter about hobbies and entertainment.
    - Writing a school magazine article.
    - Writing an e-mail to a friend saying what you want to do with your free time this weekend.
    - Writing a story for younger learners or for another audience to read.
    - Writing an account of an event or accident.

The weakness of the above is that it can leave many early level learners at the practice stage with few opportunities for real use of the language-related skills. It is important to offer communicative opportunities at all levels to maintain interest and purpose. There is a rich literature on the teaching of the four skills:

for guidance on the teaching of listening, Ur (1984), writing for English language teachers is still one of the most helpful sources, while Turner (1995) offers a guide for modern language teachers; Littlewood (1992) offers an excellent overview of how teaching can focus on the development of speaking, from the 'skill-getting' pre-communicative stages to 'skill-using' communicative activities; Grellet (1981) and Nuttall (1982, 1996) provide guidance and practical examples for the teaching of reading. In the Centre for Information on Language Teaching and Research (CILT) Pathfinder Series, Mitchell and Swarbrick (1994) and Swarbrick (1998) directly address the needs of modern foreign language teachers of reading. Writing is perhaps less well served, though again the Pathfinder Series and others offer rich sources of ideas in a range of publications, for example, Jones (1992), Miller (1995), Kavanagh and Upton (1994).

Figure 3.6 offers a simple view of the language teacher's routine concerns:

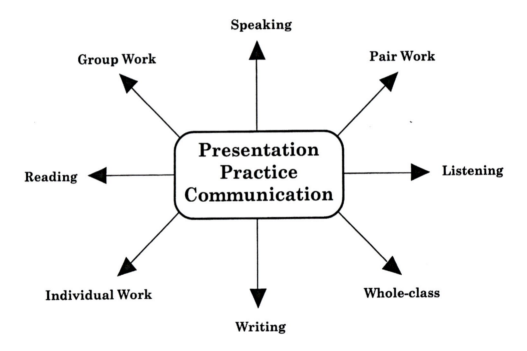

Figure 3.6

In addition, there is the continual process of preparation and evaluation of the classroom management strategies. Furthermore, other ingredients could be added: vocabulary, grammar, discourse, tests and numerous other features. As an introductory working model the above serves our purpose adequately.

Resources and strategies

A variety of well-known resources and strategies are available to assist the hard-pressed teacher at whichever stage of learning she is preparing:

Resources	Strategies
visual aids	assignments
cuecards	gesture, mime
textbooks	games
texts	drills, exercises
audio recordings, radio	role-play, simulation, drama
TV/video	tasks, activities, situations
worksheets	explanation
ICT materials, databases	
pictures	
models	
classroom	
realia; authentic material	

These are usually organised under topics, situations or themes that reflect the content of a course, scheme of work, syllabus or textbook.

Teacher qualities

A plain delivery of these strategies is clearly not enough to assure the success of language teaching – a dehumanised concentration on methodology would be enough to see off all but the most devoted of our students. To have any chance of motivating learners the teacher has to:

- present language in meaningful contexts,
- elicit language from students,
- make instructions clear to everyone,
- use a variety of techniques (cards, texts, ICT, open questions),
- manage pairs and groups to maximise practice,
- monitor individuals and groups,
- stand back and view the whole class,
- meet the needs of all, irrespective of gender or ability,
- praise warmly,
- correct when appropriate,
- confirm and welcome good use of the target language,
- smile and enjoy the job!

General qualities of sensitivity, flexibility, humour, enthusiasm and stamina (similar to those required by the average parent) inevitably affect interest and enthusiasm levels. Matthews *et al.* (1985) identify the didactic and supportive roles that teachers perform during the teaching of a language:

Stage	Teacher roles
Presentation	Informant and Motivator
Practice	Conductor and Enabler
Communication	Observer and Consultant

The changing roles reflect the principle of gradually diminishing support as teaching styles move from transmission of knowledge to facilitation and production. The teacher becomes a consultant and observer as the pupils move from being receivers to doers.

Good teachers have been described (HMIS 1987, quoted in Johnstone 1989) as 'adventurous, uncondescending, setting high expectations'. They are adventurous because they organise challenging and formative interaction, for example in simulations and other communication games. They are uncondescending because these activities are all managed without resort to put-downs, which have no place in the classroom. Put-downs lead to early drop-outs. They have high expectations because they extend pupils well beyond the endless support strategies (drills, cue-cards in English, teacher led question/answer work) that mushroomed in the 1980s.

Sensitivity to the importance of teaching and learning styles helps us to address learner needs. The importance of the learner has perhaps been understated in the past, while language specialists have been preoccupied with methodology, assuring a balance of skills, using authentic materials, including role-play, etc. The input has not always matched learner needs. Attention has now swung in the direction of the learner.

At this point, it is worthwhile recalling some of the essential qualities, many of which are considered in depth elsewhere in this book, that promote the learning of a language:

- motivation and enjoyment;
- careful planning;
- clear objectives;
- communicative purpose;
- consulting learners about their needs;
- identifying and developing good learning strategies;
- pace and variety of techniques;
- using materials appropriate to age, gender and culture;
- comprehensive initial practice on the language;
- encouragement to cope with the unpredictable;
- time to explore and experiment;
- caring, supportive, non-threatening atmosphere;
- careful monitoring of progress in learning;
- creating situations in which learners can succeed and feel self-esteem.

While the teacher has many preoccupations, learners also have concerns that condition their responses to teaching and their attitudes to learning. If we can successfully predict the features that may influence these attitudes, during preparation and evaluation, we may create healthy learning climates. Many learners will already have

- some ideas about the ways in which they can best learn,
- a fairly clear perception of their own ability,
- a battery of learning strategies,
- good or bad classroom experiences,
- expectations of what their future learning will be like.

During their language learning, they will need:

- a clear sense of purpose;
- enjoyment;
- motivation;
- success and rewards;
- support in their way of learning;
- praise;
- self-esteem;
- time.

Too much stress on the preparation of materials and methodology can lead to a failure to consider the manner in which our students learn. Taking the learners as the starting point for our efforts leads inevitably to greater importance being attached to evaluation, in particular to reviewing how much learning has taken place.

Evaluation: Looking through the eyes of the pupils

Stepping back and observing learners at work in the language classroom gives rise to the following questions (derived from the Open University model suggested in *Curriculum in Action*, Ashton *et al.* 1982):

- Which of the skills (LSRW) are being learnt, developed or practised?
- What is being learnt? Vocabulary? Transactions? Grammar?

Grammar or vocabulary can be taught by

(a) using the language;
(b) answering questions orally;
(c) writing answers to questions;
(d) asking questions.

What opportunities are made available to the pupils and what do they engage in? Do they use the language to answer questions, to ask questions, to write responses? The pupils can show they are learning by interacting purposefully, by initiating communication, by writing, by an action, by filling in a grid, by a gesture or a look.

The teacher's evaluation needs to consider the nature and quality of learning and how much success the learners enjoy in the lesson and whether the activities are sufficiently challenging for them. When the lesson has been evaluated, the key question is what next: revision, repetition of an activity, consolidation, progression to something new?

The process of evaluation does not focus in detail on subject content but primarily on the nature of the learning experience, to give clues about learner responses to what they are learning. The teacher should then ask questions about the methodology, to determine whether:

- the presentation was clear;
- practice activities had enough intrinsic purpose and time;
- the students spoke more or less than the teacher;
- there was a variety of activities;
- there was a balance of development of the four skills;
- individual learning differences were addressed and how;
- all pupils had equal opportunities to learn (for example, were boys asked to answer more than girls?)

In the next chapter, we move on to a practical exploration of the stages of language teaching identified above.

Chapter 4

Managing learning in the foreign language classroom

There are countless well-known approaches, tasks and strategies that can be employed at different stages of lessons. No single method is the best way of teaching a foreign language. Varying the approach and the task is a feature of effective teaching. With this in mind, we consider some activities that exemplify the stages already described in Chapter 3.

Presentation and initial practice

A battery of materials and strategies (some already mentioned in Chapter 3) exists to assist the presentation of language items in meaningful contexts, including for example:

Materials

OHPs	cassettes	videos
flashcards	puppets	whiteboard
pictures	texts	charts
classroom objects	real objects	computer programs

Strategies

invented stories	true stories	simulations
explanation	translation	story telling
gesture/mime	chalk and talk	working with an assistant(e)

Many of these are self-explanatory but some suggestions may help to establish ways of generating pace and interest.

Flashcards

Introducing new vocabulary or language items, see Figure 4.1 for two examples.
Particularly in the early stages of learning in primary or secondary schools, choral and individual repetition of the items allow pupils the time to gain confidence in hearing and saying the new words. Once familiarity is achieved, guessing games can be used to provide initial practice, for example:

- turning the cards round so that pupils have to guess in order to 'win' the card;
- giving pupils the cards and then using the target language to request them back;
- asking pupils to match printed labels to the flashcards.

un clavier    une souris

Figure 4.1

Real objects

(a) Pupils are invited to look at jumbled phrases on the board or flipchart and produce utterances that relate to real objects on the table in Figure 4.2.

bière   paquet chips

de   bouteille   une

un   beurre   je voudrais

lait   limonade   bonbons

s'il vous plaît

Figure 4.2

(b) Real objects can be used to present items of language, then hidden under a tablecloth, in a box, or in a bag to allow activities that involve guessing:

Qu'est-ce qu'il y a dans le sac?
Qu'est-ce qu'il y a dans la boîte/sous la nappe?

(c) Written labels can be placed on or next to real objects.

The activities outlined are tightly controlled emphasising the desire for accurate imitation and correct practice at this early stage.

Interaction with puppets/cassette player/hats

The teacher may present dialogue, structure, or language function with the aid of these materials from Key Stage 2 to Key Stage 4.

(a) Puppets act out a situational dialogue:

Puppet A:	*Bonjour, je peux vous aider?*
Puppet B:	*Oui, je voudrais visiter des caves.*
Puppet A:	*Oui, il y a un grand choix. Voici un dépliant.*
	Il y a des excursions organisées?
Puppet B:	*Est-ce que je peux réserver des places ici?*

(b) Cassette player: The same presentation effect can be achieved by pre-recording one part of the dialogue on a cassette before the lesson starts. If an FLA is available, then pre-recording is not necessary.

(c) Hat: The teacher can use a hat or a pair of sunglasses to present dialogues or assume the identity of a third person for example:

The person wearing the hat is called Alberto:

Figure 4.3

The teacher acts out some classroom activities wearing the hat thus assuming the identity of Alberto. The language is given to accompany the actions performed such as climbing on a table, getting down, leaving the room, re-entering, falling down, for example:

Alberto è salito sulla tavola.
E sceso dalla tavola.
E uscito dall'aula.
E rientrato nell'aula.
E caduto per terra.

The style of presentation may help to focus on the grammatical problem of using '*essere*' in the past (passato prossimo) in Italian or '*être*' in French.

Using a picture

Large pictures can be used in a variety of ways. For instance, a large picture of an old person is shown and the teacher elicits a description of the man using language that pupils already know:

Cet homme est vieux. Il a soixante ans. Il porte une cravate et il semble très intelligent.
Then, it is explained that the man has mysteriously disappeared:
Malheureusement, il a disparu.
The picture is hidden and a description of what he looked like is elicited or given:

Il était vieux. Il portait une cravate bleue.
Il tenait . . . Il semblait . . .

Figure 4.4

Using contrastive visuals

This useful technique can be applied to a number of situations at any secondary level, Key Stages 3 or 4:

A tidy bedroom	contrasted with	A bedroom in a state of disorder.
An old person	contrasted with	A young person.
A modern house	contrasted with	A traditional dwelling.

The opportunities for presentation and initial practice are many involving the language of:

description:	*il y a ..., la chambre est petite,* etc.
speculation/prediction:	*peut-être que la jeune n'a pas le temps pour manger ... donc, il n'y a rien sur la table ...*
comparison:	*la vieille maison a plus de charme que la moderne, mais ....,*
addition:	*en plus, la maison moderne coûte moins chère ...*

Practice activities

Traditionally, practice activities have drawn on the support of:

worksheets	diagrams	cards	cassettes	pictures	texts
cuecards	grids	games	videos	databases	charts

The use of these materials depends on the level of the group and the differentiation required. Activities based on such materials are examples of teacher-led tasks. A teacher may decide to set some of them for high achievers and others for low attainers, the choice and application depending on level and need.

A selection of the following may be organised as self-access activities, a productive way of devolving practice away from teacher-led question–answer work. This brings some variety and stimulates an atmosphere of trust and working together. All of the practice activities relate to the topic *A La Gare*.

Spell and match (Key Stage 2)

Learners spell out key words using letter cards and match them to pictures:

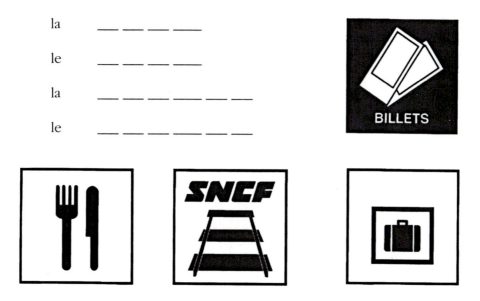

Figure 4.5

Match the word to the picture (Key Stage 2/3)

Figure 4.6 shows images with which the following words are matched:

la consigne automatique; la salle d'attente; le buffet; le bureau de renseignements

Figure 4.6

The opportunity for error is very limited as it is in the following task.

Labelling a picture (Key Stage 2/3)

Learners put labels of the following kind on to a picture of a station:

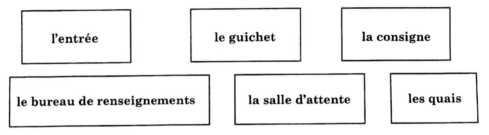

Figure 4.7

Labelling and matching activities can be expanded to include structure practice, for example, as a label or card is placed the student is required to say:

Voici le guichet.
Voici la consigne.
Or, at a higher level,
Je vais au guichet pour …
Je vais à la consigne pour …

Pouce (Key Stage 2/3)

This can be a whole-class or large group activity. Ideally, six flashcards are required for a group of fifteen to twenty pupils. It can be played with more but then some pupils may not get a turn and become restless. Pupils practise the language for each card for example:

Où est la consigne, svp? Où est le bureau de renseignements, svp? Où sont les toilettes, svp?

Six pupils are selected to hold the cards while the rest of the group hide their faces and stick a thumb in the air. Those holding cards creep round the class and each one touches one other pupil's thumb. Once touched, the pupil must put down his or her thumb so that it is not touched by another card carrier. When all the card carriers are back at the front of the group, the instructions '*Ouvrez les yeux et levez-vous si on vous a touché*' should be given.

At this stage, the 'touched' have to guess which card touched them. They are allowed to use one phrase in the foreign language which, if correct and equivalent to the card that touched them, earns them the card. They are then 'on'. Turns should be restricted to two consecutive 'goes', otherwise some pupils do not get a chance. This game is amazingly popular in the 10–13 age range and we have known difficult Year 9 pupils bay for it. It is criticised for being time-consuming in relation to the amount of language practised but pupils react very positively to the activity and seem to find it motivating. It can be used to practise any vocabulary or structure (whatever the level) provided that you have appropriate pictures or even objects. A set of animal pictures could lead to:

Je pense que c'était un – loup qui m'a attaqué.
– serpent
– chien, etc.

Confirmation should be given in the target language, i.e.:

Non, tu as tort/Oui, tu as raison, c'était un chien.

A set of activity or hobby pictures could be used to practise questions:

Est-ce que tu aimes   – faire de la natation?
– danser?
– jouer dans la rue?
– aller au théâtre?

If correctly identified the holder answers:

Oui, j'aime faire de la natation.

And, if the guess is wrong:

Non, je n'aime pas ...

In this way, Pouce promotes the target language, provided that pupils have had sufficient initial practice so that they can say the phrases. With difficult phrases, blackboard or wallchart prompts are useful supports for the forgetful (so long as they have practised reading).

Speaking table (Key Stage 3/4)

This involves role-play with information gap using a train timetable as in the illustration, Figure 4.8.

Some members of the class have this information and act as employees in the *guichet*, while others have prompt cards and are required to perform transactions and note the information, Figure 4.9.

TRAINS AU DEPART

| DESTINATION | HEURE | QUAI | TARIF   Deuxième   Classe |
			S R
Paris	1023	1	220F 400F
Toulouse	1037	2	210F 390F
Dieppe	1112	4	90F 165F
Marseille	1129	2	230F 410F
Nantes	1205	3	220F 400F
Lyon	1348	1	200F 380F

Figure 4.8

Paris	Nantes	Toulouse . . .	Marseille . . .
Heure	Heure	Heure	Heure . . . . . .
Quai	Quai	Quai	Quai . . . .
S	R	R	S . . . .

Figure 4.9

This activity is of the guided-practice type, with learners offered the chance to use the language in a restricted way. Successful completion of the transaction depends on the efficacy of the presentation and initial practice.

The information can be checked on a master board at the end of the activity. Immediate confirmation of success is valuable and early correction of misunderstandings will help students to see the future communicative value of listening for specific information. Before setting such an activity students have to be aware of the conventions used and the purposes of the task. The next stage might involve learners in the use of real timetables so that they quickly become accustomed to standard conventions.

Reading (Key Stage 3/4)

With more advanced pupils, handwritten texts or e-mails offer usefully exploitable practice material, as with the following message and picture:

Madeleine écrit un message confidentiel pour son chef de travail.

De:	*Madeleine Maurice <SEC/MM9>*
a:	*bmartin*
Date:	*lun, 25 Oct 1999 12:39:45 +0100 (HF)*
Sujet:	*Lorent*
	Brigitte,

Je suis arrivée à la gare à huit heures comme prévu. J'ai cherché mon partenaire, Lorent. J'ai regardé dans le buffet mais il n'était pas là. Que faire? Je portais des documents secrets dans la valise. Je devais cacher la valise. Donc, j'ai décidé de la mettre à la consigne automatique. J'y suis allée et j'ai trouvé un coffre vide. J'ai mis la valise et j'ai fermé la boîte à clef.

Puis, j'ai acheté un journal anglais. J'ai passé quelques minutes à lire le journal devant le kiosque, puis je suis allée vers la sortie. Soudain, j'ai vu Lorent avec deux hommes mystérieux. Que faisait Lorent? Est-ce qu'il donnait des informations? Je me suis cachée derrière l'horaire des trains car un des hommes portait un revolver ...

(a) *Tracez la route de Madeleine*

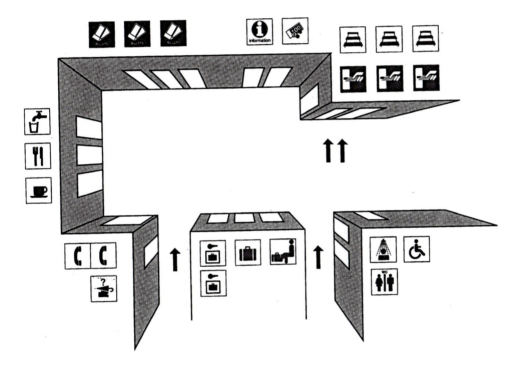

Figure 4.10

(b)   *Vrai/faux*

(i)   *Madeleine est professeur.*
(ii)   *Elle a cherché son partenaire de travail.*
(iii)   *Lorent n'était pas à la gare.*
(iv)   *Madeleine a acheté un journal espagnol.*

(c)   Pupils write an end to the story.

Alternatives could involve a series of teacher questions:

Répondez aux questions:

(i)   *Qui est le chef?*
(ii)   *Qu'est-ce que Madeleine a cherché?*
(iii)   *Où est-ce qu'elle a mis la valise?*
(iv)   *Pourquoi?*

or pictures for pupils to order in narrative sequence. The text can be cut up for pupils to sequence (jigsaw reading) or matched with pictures. Pupils could also read the story and role-play a meeting between Madeleine and her boss, before writing the end of the story.

Listening task (Key Stage 3)

Pupils listen to a series of railway station announcements and note down the information heard in the box – see, for example, Figure 4.11.

TRAINS AU DEPART

DESTINATION		HEURE	QUAI
TOULOUSE	TGV		
MARSEILLE	Express		
LYON	Rapide		
PERPIGNAN	Express		

Figure 4.11

Tables of this type are useful for the setting of information transfer tasks on listening and reading tasks. They allow pupils to make short written responses but channel them to focus on the key points when listening or reading. This provides a purpose to the listening and reading and helps pupils to process the language.

Games table (Key Stage 3/4)

(a) Board Game: see Figure 4.12. Players land on a square after the throw of a dice and have to use an utterance related to the context. A point is scored for every appropriate utterance for example:

> *Cette place est libre?*
> *Je voudrais un thé, s'il vous plaît.*

Rules creating extra challenge or difficulty can be introduced for example, no repetitions allowed, or make questions only. The pictures or squares cue the language to be used by learners, with the level of support now somewhat diminished.

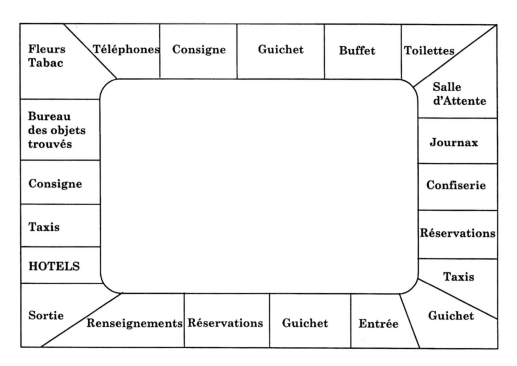

Figure 4.12

(b) Card Games: see Figure 4.13. Students turn over cue cards and perform the transactions indicated.

This is of course a practice drill but when devolved to students it can be much more useful and motivating than teacher-led practice from the front of the room. Students perform the transactions while their peers monitor and support. If it is felt appropriate students can 'win' the cue card if they make a 'correct' transaction.

Bordeaux	Paris	Paris	Lyon
l ère classe	2 ème classe	Heure?	Direct?
Aller-retour	Aller-retour	Quai?	Heure?

Toulouse	Réservations:	Réservations:	Rennes
Aller-retour	2 personnes	Une personne	2 ème classe
TGV	Narbonne	Carcassonne	Aller simple
	10 hr 23	14h 51	

Figure 4.13

During the activities, it is advisable to stand aside at regular intervals to monitor pupils' work and development. This creates an impression of encouragement and control. Intrusive interference (for example, to correct language) while pupils are performing tasks, can be demotivating. If correction is needed it might be wiser to stop an activity, give guidance and then set learners off again. Alternatively, the teacher can make a mental note of difficulties that require action and take remedial steps later.

Communicative activities

Some of the activities already listed above, for example the speaking table, are close to the communicative stage. It is difficult to establish situations for 'real' communication unless we can get our own pupils to express their own thoughts and opinions.

Sadly, the communication stage has often been mistaken for an extension of guided practice, giving rise to the endless succession of controlled role-plays visited on hordes of bewildered teenagers, as in this example below.

Buying presents

The assistant asks if he can help you.
Reply that you are looking for a present for your brother.
He asks how old he is.
You say that he is nearly ten years old.
He shows you some games.
Explain that your brother is not interested in games.

Perhaps, there is a place for this type of practice but the demands rarely go beyond the mechanical and transactional. It presents the first stage in the development of role-play skills. However, role-play can be come a sterile activity if pupils are not encouraged to go beyond this stage. An obvious improvement would be to have students using authentic materials in reasonably realistic simulations that offer them opportunities for:

● spontaneous use of the target language to cope with the unexpected;
● information gap activities;
● sending messages;
● formulating responses to stimuli;
● reading authentic materials, stories, poetry;
● listening to native speech, even songs.

Role-play (Key Stage 4)

This activity works best with real timetables and if possible some sort of simulated telephone link. A French assistant is also very useful as the *Employé*! A preparation for this would be to see or hear French people coping with a similar situation. If this is not possible the teacher can simulate the experience by acting the first role and pre-recording the other roles on cassette recorders. Relevant rail timetables are required for this activity.

Parisien(ne):

Tu habites à Paris. Ton amie te téléphoné pour te dire qu'il y a un problème et que tu dois aller tout de suite à Rouen par le premier train possible. Note l'heure du départ du train, l'heure d'arrivée, achète un billet aller-retour. Puis téléphone à ton ami(e) à Rouen pour lui dire à quelle heure tu arrives.

Employé(e):

Consulte les horaires et donne les renseignements demandés. Il y aura des voyageurs pour Strasbourg, Rouen, Metz et Calais.

Ami(e):

Tu habites à Rouen. Téléphone à ton ami(e) à Paris pour lui dire qu'il y a un problème et tu veux que l'ami(e) vienne à Rouen (for example, *un cambrioleur a volé tout ton argent*).

Reading for information (Key Stage 4)

In the language classroom, reading is often used for language learning purposes and little else. We suggest that pupils need to practise reading the foreign language, for meaning and communication, for information, for pleasure. Tasks that develop skills of skimming, scanning, reading for meaning should be encouraged. Check questions may follow in English or in the target language, depending on the level of pupil confidence and skill. A simple example follows.

TER Pass Bretagne

Vous êtes en vacances avec des amis. Lisez le text et expliquez les possibilités à vos copains:

Profitez des longues journées d'été

Prix ....

Période valable ....

Jour valable ....

Transports possibles ....

Nombre de trajets possibles ....

Où acheter un billet? ....

TER PASS BRETAGNE 60 F POUR VOYAGER LES SAMEDIS D'ÉTÉ

Du 26 juin au 18 septembre, élargissez votre horizon et sillonnez la Bretagne de long en large pendant les samedis d'été.

Vous voulez faire dans la journée autant de trajets que vous le désirez ? Pour 60 F, le Pass Bretagne vous donne accès à tous les trains et cars TER.

Que de beaux samedis d'été en perspective !

Renseignez-vous dans les gares et boutiques SNCF ou téléphonez au 08 36 35 35 35 (2F23 la minute) ou consultez le 3615 TER (1F01 la minute).

Informations non contractuelles, données sous réserve de modifications ultérieures à l'édition du présent document. Prix au 01JO2J99.

À NOUS DE VOUS FAIRE PRÉFÉRER LE TER.

Figure 4.14

Listening for communicative purposes (Key Stage 4)

This activity requires careful preparation. It can depend on students asking questions to find out about available accommodation from someone holding the required information. Or, it can be done by means of listening inputs if available. Textbooks offer a range of such possibilities. The following is an example of the approach for more able pupils.

Some friends are looking for a flat. They each make (telephone) enquiries and then meet to discuss possibilities.

Ecoutez les textes et écrivez les informations que vous recevez dans les cases suivantes:

Adresse	5 Rue V. Hugo	10 Rue Prévert	25 Rue Mérimé	30 Rue St Jacques
Etage				
Chauffage				
Nombre de pièces				
Téléphone				
Loyer				
Autres détails intéressants				

Figure 4.15

The texts to which pupils listen can be of the following type:

Texte 1	Texte 2
Allô, c'est bien 5 Rue Victor Hugo? Eh, oui, c'est ça. Et alors, madame, vous avez un appartement à louer? Oui, ça vous intéresse? Ça dépend. C'est à quel étage? Au second étage d'un petit immeuble, monsieur. Il est vide. Ah oui, et il a le chauffage central? Bien sur, chauffage central électrique, mais ce n'est pas compris dans le loyer. Chauffage central électrique, chauffage central électrique ... et le loyer, vous avez dit, c'est combien par mois? 5000 FF par mois, mais il y a deux chambres et c'est tout meublé. C'est un appartement assez moderne, monsieur, construit dans les années soixante; quatre pièces, plus la salle de bains avec douche. Il y a deux chambres, une grande cuisine et un salon. Il y a aussi le téléphone, un balcon et vous avez accès à un parking privé garanti. Et madame, ça se trouve où exactement? En banlieue, monsieur, dans un quartier tranquille. C'est calme ici. 5000 FF par mois, OK. Vous habitez dans le même quartier? Oui, monsieur, nous habitons au rez-de-chaussée du même immeuble. Mais, on ne vous dérangerait pas. Vous avez une entrée privée. Alors, est-ce que je peux vous rendre visite pour voir l'appartement, voir si ça me convient? ...	Allô, c'est bien 30 Rue St Jacques? Pas exactement, mais je suis le propriétaire. Et alors, monsieur, vous avez un studio à louer? Oui, c'est ça. C'est à quel étage? Au second étage d'un immeuble à six étages, monsieur. Il sera vide dans deux semaines. Ah oui, et il a quelle sorte de chauffage? Chauffage central électrique, mais ce n'est pas compris dans le loyer. Chauffage central électrique, chauffage central électrique ... et le loyer c'est combien par mois? 4000 FF par mois. Quatre milles ... Il y a combien de pièces? Il y a une chambre et c'est tout meublé. C'est un studio très moderne, construit il y a cinq ou six ans, monsieur, avec douche et une cuisine séparée. Il y a aussi le téléphone, et vous avez droit au parking dans la rue. Et madame, ça se trouve où exactement? Près du centre de la ville, monsieur, dans un quartier intéressant. Ce n'est pas loin du cinéma Gaumont, si vous connaissez le centre. Vous habitez dans le même quartier? Non, monsieur, nous habitons en banlieue. On ne vous dérangerait pas. Alors, est-ce que je peux vous rendre visite pour voir si ça me convient? ...

Each pupil could listen to the two conversations (or makes two phone calls). Then, pupils are paired so they can meet to discuss preferences. These can be limited by true/false questions of the following type:

(a) *5 Rue V. Hugo est plus moderne que 30 Rue St Jacques.*
(b) *5 Rue V. Hugo coûte plus cher que 30 Rue St Jacques.*
(c) *Rue St Jacques se trouve dans un quartier plus calme que les autres.*
(d) *30 Rue St Jacques coûte moins cher que tous les autres appartements.*

Or, the following specifications are given to the pupils taking part. They listen and determine which flat is suitable and write down why.

Vous voulez deux chambres et vous préférez la tranquillité et les conforts modernes (douches, balcon, chauffage central, téléphone etc.). Vous n'aimez pas les animaux. Vous voulez dépenser à peu près 5000 FF en loyer.

If a listening input is not possible for this task, an alternative is to give each participant two written descriptions of the flats and then allow them to meet to compare notes and swap information.

Letter writing

Traditionally, letter writing has formed part of the staple diet of the writing syllabus, with opportunities for writing letters in response to adverts for jobs, (Key Stage 4 and sixth form), in response to advertisements for pen-friends (any stage). There has often been encouragement to provide learners with real audiences for their letter writing, for example, for class-to-class exchanges with a school in the target language country. This latter is now much easier through e-mail though the kind of writing needed for e-mail correspondence is not the same as informal letter writing. As styles of writing by e-mail settle down, language teachers will need to give careful attention to the form and levels of formality that become standard. The key to successful writing is adequate preparation at the pre-writing phase, identifying the purpose, audience, form and content of the writing. Pre-writing oral work is often the crucial element in the teacher's guidance for learners' writing.

Interview simulation (Key Stage 4 and Years 12–13)

Authentic sources can offer the stimulus material for this activity: pop stars, sports people, film stars often appear in magazine interviews or biographies from which a simulation similar to the following can be performed in groups of three – presenter, interviewer and interviewee. If the personality is of interest to the students the activity is creative and motivating because they use their reading and listening for communicative purposes. At the preparation stage, pupils might assign strips of dialogue to a series of cartoons of interviewer and interviewee; or order snippets of discourse in a conversation script as found in magazines or on radio. The following is an example of how the simulation can be structured. Ideally, learners would have access to biographical details of people likely to appeal to their interests, for example, actors, singers, sports personalities.

Présentateur: Il est huit heures. Maintenant, l'entrevue avec Sembène Ousmane, l'écrivain sénégalais ...

Intervieweur: Bonjour, ...

Sembène Ousmane:

[After guided preparation, potential interviewers work together in small groups to devise appropriate questions.]

Interviewer

Vous allez faire une entrevue avec l'écrivain sénégalais, Sembène Ousmane. Il est bien connu en France pour ses deux romans: 'Le Docker Noir' et 'Oh, pays, mon beau peuple'. Il a écrit beaucoup d'autres livres. L'écrivain fait un tour de promotion en France.

Dans votre groupe, préparez des questions pour apprendre les détails de la vie de Sembène: lieu de naissance, âge, parents, sa vie d'enfant, collège, premier travail, etc. Préparez des questions sur sa vie en France (quand, où, pourquoi?) et sur sa famille. Naturellement, posez des questions sur les livres de Sembène et essayez de découvrir ce que Sembène fait à part l'écriture.

(a) Préparez les questions.

(b) Trouvez votre 'Sembène'. Introduisez l'émission de radio et présentez Sembène aux auditeurs. Faites l'entrevue.

(c) Finissez le programme avec une conclusion.

The pupil(s) taking the role of the writer Sembène Ousmane have the following information:

Vous jouez le rôle de Sembène Ousmane. On va vous poser des questions sur votre vie et votre carrière. Préparez des réponses surtout en ce qui concerne:

parents, vie d'enfance, travail, vie en France, famille, livres, autre travail, autres activités.

Nom:	*Sembène Ousmane*
An de naissance:	*1923*
Lieu de naissance:	*Un village près de Dakar, au Sénégal, Afrique de l'Ouest.*
Enfance:	*Ecole Primaire. Pas de Collège Secondaire. Enfance normale, mais pauvre. Pourtant, il aimait lire.*

Travail:	*Pêcheur à l'âge de 15 ans, comme son père. Puis, maçon et plombier.*
1939-45	*Deuxième Guerre Mondiale – soldat, Armée Française en Italie et Allemagne.*
1945	*Retourne au Sénégal. Pas satisfait. Il voulait écrire mais c'était difficile pour un Sénégalais. Donc, retourne en France, à Marseille. Docker dans le port de Marseille et membre du parti communiste. Il a commencé à écrire.*
1956	*Publication du roman 'Le Docker Noir' (basé sur les experiences de Sembène à Marseille).*
1957	*'Oh, pays, mon beau peuple' publié. Ce roman décrit les problèmes de reintégration à la société traditionnelle sénégalaise. Un sénégalais est retourné avec une femme française et de nouvelles idées. Ça cause des problèmes dans le village.*
1964	*Publication de 'l'Harmattan'. Puis, Sembène est allé à Moscou et il est devenu directeur de films.*
Autres détails:	*Beaucoup d'autres romans, par exemple, 'Le Mandat', 'Xala'. Et, il a fait des films de ces romans. 'Le Mandat' a gagné un prix au Festival de Films à Venise, en Italie. Il a beaucoup voyagé partout dans le monde. Il aime voyager, le théâtre, le cinéma et l'Afrique.*

Story activities

All children from an early age like to listen to stories. By telling stories the teacher can develop the pupils' own linguistic and creative skills. Examples of approaches, derived from the literature on English language teaching, can be found in Morgan and Rinvolucri (1984), Wright (1995) and other sources, for example:

(a)   a regular serial story, which is continued from lesson to lesson;
(b)   a dungeons and dragons story, which begins:
        J'arrive devant le château et j'entre par la grande porte ...
        The pupils continue, while the teacher draws arrows, diagrams and pictures on the board in response to their prompts;
(c)   a complicated picture for each pupil, accompanied by an extensive set of questions on it, either on tape or in writing. The pupils cross out or erase the questions they do not want to use and then construct a story based on the picture;
(d)   the teacher starts the story with a sentence or a phrase and each pupil in turn adds a phrase or sentence.

The use of stories in the language classroom received growing interest in the 1990s, for example, Wright (1995) on English language stories for young children. *Cric-Crac!* (Dunning 1997) offers a wealth of ideas as well as a number of old favourite stories in French versions, for example *La soupe au caillou* (1997, pp. 83–4). Dunning shows how stories can be used at all school levels from Key Stage 3 to A Level.

Some of the benefits for using storytelling in the classroom include:

- The enjoyment and psychological benefits of working with stories can build confidence and increase motivation for both teachers and learners. The opportunities for collaborating in the development of stories are endless and provide a non-threatening way of allowing individual responses, partnerships and choral speaking.
- Stories can be shortened, lengthened, have characters and elements changed, be anything from a paragraph to a lengthy book.
- The content of stories can be explored and a large number of exploitation activities can be set up in the telling or reading and as follow-up.

Storytelling provides valuable opportunities for listening as well as speaking. It can lead to other activities: project work; role-play; writing stories for a class library or for younger learners. It is a valuable aid to the teaching of literacy in the foreign language and contributes to the development of other skills (notably listening and speaking). Before hearing or reading stories pupils can engage in brainstorming or scene-setting activities. Teachers help by organising vocabulary elicitation activities that focus on topic-related key words (colours, animals, personal qualities, food, etc.).

Stories can be effective even in Key Stages 2 and 3 where pupils can be asked to listen and respond to stories (for example, fairy stories, anecdotes, daily routines) before seeking to re-tell them, first orally then in writing. Story work sensitises learners to the nature of language, for example the grammatical and the stylistic. It offers an integrated way of dealing with all four skills, initially listening and speaking, laying foundations and providing contexts for reading and writing. Pupils can also learn about expressiveness in the voice, about patterns of intonation which should influence their own attempts to read the target language.

Teachers can organise a range of activities with stories: reading and sequencing the story text, matching text to pictures, giving titles to parts of stories, dictation of a part of the story, question and answer work, listening to most of the story and being asked to predict different endings, listening to the story then engaging in a role-play.

The following example of a story is translated and adapted from a pack of materials issued by the Leicestershire Multicultural Resource Centre. The French version has been used successfully with children and adults.

Un lion vaniteux

Milord Rex était un lion. C'était un très beau lion, fier et féroce. Un jour il a décidé de faire une promenade. D'abord, il a rencontré un papillon.

– *'Quelles belles ailes tu as', a dit Milord Rex.*

   'Si seulement j'avais des ailes comme toi.'
– *'Je suis un papillon magique', a répondu le papillon. 'Tu peux avoir ce que tu désires.'*

Soudain, de très belles ailes ont poussé sur le dos du lion. Elles battaient sur ses côtés. Elles se déployaient dans le vent. Le lion était très content. Il pouvait voler. Mais, au bout d'un certain moment, il s'est impatienté. Petit à petit, il s'ennuyait. Puis, il a rencontré un kangourou.

– *'Quelles belles pattes de derrière tu as', a dit Milord Rex! 'Si seulement, j'avais des pattes de derrière comme toi.'*
– *'Je suis un kangourou magique', a répondu le kangourou. 'Tu peux avoir ce que tu désires.'*

Soudain, les pattes du lion ont poussé. Il avait de fortes et longues pattes de derrière. Il sautait, il bondissait. Il était très content. Mais, au bout d'un certain moment, il s'est impatienté. Petit à petit, il s'ennuyait. Ensuite, il a rencontré un éléphant.

– *'Quelle belle trompe tu as', a dit Milord Rex. 'Si seulement j'avais une trompe comme toi.'*
– *'Je suis un éléphant magique', a répondu l'éléphant. 'Tu peux avoir ce que tu désires.'*

Soudain, une longue trompe a poussé sur le museau du lion. Elle était longue et flexible. Le lion pouvait se gratter le dos et pouvait boire facilement dans les rivières. Il ramassait les fruits. Il était très content. Mais au bout d'un certain moment, il s'est impatienté. Petit à petit, il s'ennuyait. Après cela, il a rencontré un oiseau.

– *'Quelle belles plumes tu as', a dit le lion.*
   'Si seulement j'avais des plumes comme toi.'
– *'Je suis un oiseau magique', a répondu l'oiseau. 'Tu peux avoir ce que tu désires.'*

Soudain, la queue du lion a poussé de belles plumes. Elles étaient très jolies, de toutes les couleurs. Milord Rex marchait fièrement dans la forêt tout en regardant sa jolie queue. Le lion était très content. Mais au bout d'un certain moment, il s'est impatienté. Petit à petit, il s'ennuyait. Enfin, il a rencontré une giraffe.

– *'Quel beau cou tu as', a dit Milord Rex.*
   'Si seulement j'avais un cou comme toi.'
– *'Je suis une giraffe magique', a répondu la giraffe. 'Tu peux avoir ce que tu désires.'*

Soudain le cou du lion s'est allongé. C'était fantastique parce que le lion pouvait regarder au loin, par dessus les arbres et voir ses ennemis approcher. Milord Rex était très content. Maintenant, il avait de belles ailes, deux grandes pattes de derrière, une longue trompe, de belles plumes et un très long cou.

C'était un animal très impressionnant.

Un jour, Milord Rex est arrivé au bord d'un lac. Il s'est regardé dans l'eau. Quelle horreur!

– *'Aaaaaaaaaah! Que je suis laid!' a-t-il crié.*

Un peu plus tard, il a rencontré un autre lion. Ce lion lui a demandé:

– *'Tu es quoi comme animal?'*
– *'J'étais un lion comme toi, mais je voulais être différent', a répondu Milord Rex. 'Si seulement j'étais normal comme toi.'*
– *'Je suis un lion magique', a dit le lion. 'Tu peux avoir ce que tu désires.'*
Soudain, Milord Rex s'est transformé. Ses ailes ont disparu. Ses pattes ont diminué. Son museau s'est reformé. Son cou a rétréci. Les plumes ont disparu. Encore une fois, Milord Rex était très content. Tous les jours il retourne au lac, se regarde dans l'eau et sourit.

The above text can be used in a variety of ways. Pupils can:

- listen to or read the story and try to draw what the lion looks like at each stage;
- sequence pictures (if available) or sequence a cut-up text;
- role-play the different meetings of the lion and other animals;
- complete a range of tasks, from controlled to freer forms of writing, for example, gap-filling, transferring information to a table, identifying adjectives that describe parts of the body;
- be given the opening and closing paragraphs and then write the middle, about the meetings with the kangaroo, elephant, bird and giraffe.

The possibilities are enormous. Stories that a teacher knows can be woven into a language course. Consider stories that incorporate repetition of language items and structures, as with the text above. If you can bring one to mind, you may be able to use it for the teaching of grammar, for instance a foreign language version of *The Very Hungry Caterpillar* (Eric Carle 1969) told in the present tense could contribute to development of language, notably: numbers, days of the week, animals, food, third-person singular present tense verbs. Interest in the use of stories at primary level has grown in recent times as evidenced by the *Primary Storytelling Resource Pack*, built around two stories in French: The Giant Turnip and Goldilocks (Tierney and Humphreys, 1999). For primary school teachers, Tierney and Dobson (1995) demonstrate how traditional stories can be used in the early stages of learning a foreign language. Stories can be found from a variety of sources. For example, Revell and Norman (1997, pp. 135–6) in their book on Neurolinguistic Programming (NLP) offer an excellent example for more able students with a story called *The Wise Teacher and the Jar.*

Writing stories can also be used at a variety of levels to develop both oral and literacy skills. Pupils in pairs can compose a story for reading by others in class, school or exchange school, perhaps guided by a set of pictures or a writing frame of some kind, for example (Key Stage 4 or Years 12–13):

Voici les ingrédients d'une histoire. Remplissez les ingrédients avec vos idées. Puis, avec un partenaire, construisez une histoire:

Le jour/le temps   _____

Description du héros/de l'héroïne
(for example, un roi âgé;
nom, âge, physique, etc.)   _____

Le nom d'un(e) ami(e)   _____

Traits de l'ami(e)   _____

Description de la mauvaise
personne/du problème   _____

Détails par exemple, les vêtements
que porte la mauvaise personne;
la situation dangereuse   _____

Le danger dans lequel le héros/
l'héroïne se trouve   _____

La solution/conclusion   _____

Pictures can be used to structure the writing activity from the pre-writing oral preparation phase through to the writing task itself. The writing task can be quite open or tightly structured (gap-filling, paragraph completion or writing the ending to a story). Completed stories are proofread, shared or displayed. If writing is the principal objective it is important that any writing attempted by learners is carefully prepared at the pre-writing phase (with oral work and practice of structures to focus on language, and working out the purpose and audience for the text to focus on the writing process).

If e-mail facilities are available, stories, letters, accounts and articles can find an immediate audience with a target language school that is willing to exchange such materials. During all of these activities the teacher acts as organiser and expert consultant. To assure adequate classroom control, planning has to be thorough and done well in advance. One's relationship with the class will determine the scope and ambition of communicative activities. Well-prepared students who understand and sympathise with the learning purpose will respond creatively and sensibly to the responsibility for learning implicit in the structure and context of communicative activities.

Further examples of communicative activities occur throughout the book where they relate to the development of positive learner strategies, the teaching of grammar and vocabulary, and the preparation of teaching materials.

Chapter 5

Learning to learn a language

Pupils express views about learning:

'I learn better when I can see the words.'
'I learn from my mistakes.'
'I learn better when the teacher explains things.'
'I like to work it out in my head before I have to say anything.'
'I like to play games, without the teacher always interfering.'

Many teachers yearn for groups of pupils who

- are willing to listen and speak;
- are not discouraged by errors in speech;
- learn from mistakes;
- practise as often as possible;
- are mentally active;
- think in the target language;
- find ways of learning language patterns and vocabulary!
- review their own progress.

Such a picture of commitment and confidence would encourage any teacher.

Focus on the learner

A lot of recent attention has focused on learner training and personal strategies for learning, for example, Buckby *et al.* (1992), Grenfell and Harris (1993, 1994, 1998, 1999), Harris (1997), Macaro (1998), and Graham (1997) on how sixth form students use language learning strategies. Despite the uncertainty of our thinking about the way people learn, this development of interest is of great potential benefit to our pupils, perhaps leading them to a greater understanding of how to learn and how to respond to difficulties in learning.

For the majority of people, learning appears to be a rather uneven experience. The first National Curriculum Working Party acknowledged that learning a language is a non-linear 'uneven process' (DES 1990, 4.14) and recognised that 'learners need to feel that they have some control over their own learning.' (9.13).

Other influences support this tentative but healthy focus on the learner. Records of Achievement and Action Planning provide frequent opportunities for review, self-assessment and target-setting. Inevitably, such conscious reflection on the part of pupils and teachers must involve consideration of learning styles and preferred techniques for learning a language.

What makes a good learner?

Sadly, we are still a fair way from finding a comprehensive answer to this question. However, there has been much helpful investigation in recent years and courses in learner training have begun to emerge. Ellis and Sinclair (1989, pp. 6–7) have summarised what are believed to be some general characteristics of 'good learners'. They stress that there is no magic formula but evidence suggests that good learners tend to:

- be aware of their own positive/negative feelings to learning;
- have a genuine interest in learning the language;
- want to find out more about the language;
- monitor and assess their own progress;
- set themselves attainable short-term objectives;
- explore strategies to find ones that best suit them;
- take risks by experimenting with the language;
- organise their time effectively;
- use resources available to them both in and outside of the classroom;
- have high self-esteem.

If these qualities are desirable, the challenge is to foster them in the secondary classroom. Pupils are thoughtful people who bring a range of personal learning strategies to the task of coping with the curricular demands made on them.

However, there is evidence that some learners do not have positive strategies to assist their learning. Grenfell and Harris (1993) studied one hundred 11–14-year-old language learners and identified deficiencies that inhibit not only language development but also limit a range of other important cognitive and social-interactive strategies. They discovered:

- a failure to use the target language as often as possible, a particular failing when pupils were not directly engaged in a teacher supervised controlled task;
- a deficiency in study skills, for example, a lack of quick reference skills;
- deficiencies in social-interactive skills, particularly group work.

There have been developments in learner training which offer some promise. Macaro (1998) suggests that boys in particular benefit from learner training. Given the anxiety caused by boys' underachievement since the 1970s (regularly documented in HMI inspection reports and articles, for example, Dobson 1998, p. 9, Barton 1997, and Place 1997), a creative and cooperative exploration of approaches that enhance learning could be beneficial. Through teacher reviews and pupil reviews of their own learning perhaps effective ways of language learning can be explored and encouraged over the length of a secondary school course, normally five years. Effective strategies to promote might include:

1. General private strategies

- Planning;
- Organisation of time;
- Use of resources, including a computer for re-drafting;
- Review of achievement;
- Selection of priorities.

2. Language-specific strategies

- Repetition of words and phrases;
- Mouthing of words and phrases;
- Silent practice (rehearsing in one's head, inner speech);
- Loud practice (rehearsal of dialogues, for example);
- Classifying language items to assist learning (for example, vocabulary);
- Using prior knowledge or 'knowledge of the world' to help understanding;
- Experimenting with language;
- Applying rules;
- Note-taking and reviewing one's notes;
- Guessing or inferring meanings;
- Translation;
- Using a computer for re-drafting.

3. Settings for interactive strategies

- Pair work/group work;
- Working with the teacher in the classroom;
- Learning from a native speaker (conversation classes);
- Group projects and problem-solving;
- Foreign language days (for example, Miniville);
- Visits or exchanges to target language countries;
- Group or pair review of learning;
- E-mail communications;
- Discussion lists, chat-lines;
- Visiting web sites for language experience, topic research for sixth form projects.

Some of the general private strategies listed may be promoted by schools in a cross-curricular way. The techniques more specific though not exclusive to foreign language learning need to be promoted from the beginning of a pupil's language study, for example, inferring meaning from text, using cognates to guess meanings. Some school departments begin this training through language awareness courses. An effective and continuing investigation into the nature of language learning may help to create greater self-awareness in learners.

Implications for pupils

Reflection on the nature of language learning and individual responses to the task should improve learning at all levels. Engaging in discussion about the aims of learning and their personal strategies leads pupils to a more active and committed involvement. This boosts motivation and fosters the qualities of self-awareness, confidence, self-esteem, realism, responsibility, organisation and independence, all identified as keys to 'good learning'.

Furthermore, there is evidence that language learners in our schools are able to produce language for set situations but cannot modify the language for use in anything other than a learned context (Johnstone 1989). With greater self-managed learning and more understanding of the goals of learning, we may be able to move away from this situation. Recent reforms have not brought a complete answer. The GCSE introduced in 1988 was often interpreted as a list of discrete speech acts to be ticked off as they are 'done', an approach which gives little encouragement to skills of analysis, problem-solving, risk-taking and experimentation. The revised GCSE, with its greater focus on the use of target language, may prove to be a vehicle to address this issue, though the examinations set in 1998 and 1999 proved disappointingly similar to their transaction-focused predecessors.

Creating an awareness in learners of the features believed to help learning may be a useful starting point. They should know that

- language learning is an uneven process;
- repetition may be helpful, especially for boys;
- it is good to experiment, so long as the learning environment is safe;
- learners need to use opportunities to practise;
- discussing their learning with others is helpful;
- guessing techniques are useful.

They may already possess some very useful learning techniques such as note-taking, strategies for understanding written language and possibly even some techniques to aid memorisation.

Implications for teachers

Active involvement in the learning process engages teachers and children in a cooperative quest to exploit and extend the range of personal learning strategies that pupils use. We have suggested that much of this development can be aided by the procedures for reviewing and recording achievement already established in schools.

This is not to advocate a bureaucratic, paper-heavy approach, but a continuing discussion about goals of learning and how best to achieve them. One practical consequence of this might be that pupils maintain a section of their file/exercise book for the noting of useful learning strategies or homework tasks, for example, on the topic of Health:

(a) Make a home wallchart for parts of the body or expressions of pain.
(b) Scan two pages of a newspaper/magazine and note any uses of health-related vocabulary.
(c) Imagine pains in different parts of the body and recall ways of explaining what is wrong.

In discussion, pupils will almost certainly come up with ideas which suit the ways they feel they best learn.

An increasing emphasis on learner training inevitably influences course planning. Schemes of work that aim to produce independent and resourceful users of a foreign language provide opportunities for:

- consideration of socio-linguistic perspectives such as register and appropriacy of language;
- the use of a range of resources such as textbooks, dictionaries, reference works;
- a focus on language learning skills, particularly listening and inferencing;
- using context to assist understanding;
- reflection on nature of the foreign language.

Such features are not bolt-on extras but features of everyday approaches in the classroom. They were perhaps not adequately encouraged by the 'role-play' dominated lessons which emerged in the 1980s, with their emphasis on the language of transactions. This is not to say that role-play has to be prescriptive and repetitive. It can be imaginative and stimulating (Maley and Duff 1982). Truly creative role-play has participants struggling to use language in collaboration to solve a problem, at a particular moment in time (accident, complaint, intrusion, something unexpected) and it moves beyond the prescribed role-play, which is not much more than a rough translation exercise. This activity leads to learning language, rather than the parroting of pre-learned transactional phrases.

The formative role of error

Given that learning a new language is a bumpy process, positive responses to error are vital to the confidence and security of young learners. There is nothing wrong with getting it wrong, if learners can then go on to learn from mistakes. If we ask learners to experiment with language, it would be very damaging to comment negatively or use dismissive gestures. Rather, the place of error as a progressive step on the way to acquisition needs to be explained to pupils and re-inforced at regular intervals in a course of study.

Tolerance of error in speaking appears to be common among the majority of native speakers who are not irretrievably irritated by mistakes (Littlewood 1984, p. 88). Indeed, the 'sympathetic native speaker' often seems more humane and supportive than many non-native teachers. Learners at all levels from Year 7 to Year 13 can succeed in communicating. Their ability to communicate should be recognised wherever possible, even when error correction is taking place.

Variety

Concentration spans and the range of ability in any class inevitably influence the choices made on presentation techniques, methods of explanation, use of instructions. When planning units of work, it is wise to review the frequency of use of techniques, approaches and resources to see that interest is not killed off. Using the OHP every lesson may encourage teacher-dominated transmission, while unremitting use of dialogues will certainly deter even the most docile of learners. In addition, Littlewood (1984, pp. 32–3) warns against over-emphasis on one particular feature of the language as this may cause over-generalisation, as in the error '*Il y en a deux hommes*'.

Occasionally, there are opportunities for 'authentic' listening, for example, to songs at the beginning of lessons as pupils enter, or to a native speaker on an aspect of foreign culture. If available, video or satellite TV can provide illuminating glimpses of life in the country of the target language and offer chances to hear and see the language in 'real' use.

Learner needs

In a learner-centred approach, perhaps the most difficult task for the teacher is to discover and meet individual learning differences. Some pupils require visual support, others like to write, while others may respond best to learning by discovering rules. There are some students who claim that they like to be told the rule or system and allowed to 'get on with it'. Some learners will want to produce the language, repeat what they hear, mouth new phrases, learn by doing, while others may prefer silent, thoughtful processing.

Differentiation has often been seen as the answer to all needs. However, it is not always clear just what is meant. It is difficult for teachers to provide individually tailored tasks and worksheets, though differentiation by task is clearly something that teachers should be able to offer occasionally to groups of learners. Differentiation by planning is also a possibility, with the teacher planning approaches to suit different learners, for example, oral questions on a text targeted at different levels. Careful planning of what to ask of whom can make for very positive outcomes in the classroom. In addition, there is differentiation by outcome or by response, where the teacher prepares general activities expecting and appreciating different levels of outcome. These outcomes are not necessarily written. Interactive speaking activities with clearly defined roles for participants, for example simulations, should be designed to allow all pupils to contribute according to ability.

Teachers are learners constantly picking up signals that give clues to the kind of strategies that their pupils most appreciate. The task is then to assure a balance of approaches that give some scope to the expression of learning preferences.

At the planning stage, some useful questions can be posed:

● What are the most appropriate strategies of presentation for the learner? (Often not the easiest for the teacher.)

- How much time do learners need for practice activities?
- What support is required – from the teacher, through resources?
- What difficulties are anticipated for different learners?
- Which learners need more support?

Differentiation can also occur through the process we expect pupils to be involved in. Different pupils flourish in different learning environments (see Chapter 1). The Neurolinguistic Programming (NLP) approach to differentiation stresses the importance of drawing on all five senses in the learning situation, especially the auditory, visual and kinaesthetic senses (hearing, seeing and touching). In any one classroom, there will be pupils who learn most effectively by hearing, or by seeing or by doing something. Lesson planing will benefit by incorporating opportunities for all three forms of learning (see Revell and Norman, 1997, for a wealth of ideas derived from NLP).

Revision

Since there is little time for frequent revision in the classroom, teachers can usefully discuss with their pupils the best ways to use their own study or homework time. This will not only allow for consolidation but also give a guided opportunity for learners to experiment and develop some control over their own learning. Though we realise that younger learners may be unwilling to adopt this approach, pupils at critical points in their secondary education may welcome guidance and act upon it. Possible strategies can be offered with pupils encouraged to use the ones they feel will be most effective for their learning:

- making a revision wallchart for homework, for example of a key pattern like the 'going to' future, or of a plan or record of one's week, as in Figure 5.1;

	matin	après-midi	soir
lundi			
mardi			
mercredi			

Figure 5.1

- making materials or posters for display in school;
- recording vocabulary on cassette for occasional listening;
- displaying key phrases or patterns in one's room or work area;
- paired reading (lunch-time club?);
- maintaining a revision section in an exercise book;
- conscious thinking in the language;
- skimming through texts to identify examples of known patterns;
- reading dialogues or conversations aloud.

Many of the above activities can, with pupil cooperation, be set for homework where home circumstances permit. For pupils without access to a cassette player perhaps a short-loan policy can be introduced to assist the development of listening strategies. Access to computers during lunch-times and through after-school homework clubs offers further self-access opportunities.

Promoting a culture of revision is time well spent and lessons that start with a quick whole-class revision activity, for example eliciting recently taught words and phrases, help pupils to focus their own revision activities.

Developing learning skills

The Modern Foreign Languages for Ages 11–16 proposals (DES 1990, 3.2) described one of the educational purposes of foreign language teaching: 'to promote learning of skills of more general application (for example, analysis, memorising, drawing of inferences).' On study skills, the Proposals identified (3.3) 'attention to general and detailed meaning in listening and reading; predicting, selecting, comparing and interpreting information; and memorisation.' These general principles remain relevant. They are repeated in revised GCSE specifications, for example, Northern Examinations and Assessment Board (GCSE Italian, Syllabus 1221, 1998).

We may recall staffroom complaints of learners' inability to remember, to infer and to analyse, but how many schemes of work are consciously designed to seek these outcomes? Ideally, teachers will want to promote learning habits that their pupils find supportive and effective. Rubin (1981) suggests that good learners of language:

- seek clarification or verification for their attempts;
- use guessing and inferencing techniques;
- explore the language to make discoveries;
- practise regularly (repetition, imitation, rehearsal);
- memorise;
- monitor and evaluate what they do.

If these approaches contribute to greater learning, it is reasonable to predict that tasks involving guessing, prediction, learning by heart, learning patterns and formulae and analysis activities will enhance learning across the ability range.

This chapter concludes with some practical suggestions that might lead to the exploration of appropriate learning techniques of general, language-specific and interactive value. None of the tasks is new but they do seem to accord with features that characterise good learning as far as we know it.

1. General strategies

Pupils of differing abilities at secondary level are likely to suggest organisational techniques they know to be of benefit to them. Ideas that we have come across include:

- pupils given a topic heading predict the language items and patterns they think they will need to communicate in this area (thus helping to plan the content and set objectives);
- keeping an index of grammar points;
- setting aside regular times for review of file/exercise book contents, for example 15 minutes per week;
- organising new language items according to theme or topic;
- referring to old exercise books and noting the contents;
- organising vocabulary notebooks by topic to enable easy access;
- making a positive review by noting all the things you can do in a particular area of the language;
- thinking positively, avoiding 'I can't do anything' responses;
- using checklists to monitor progress;
- marking one's own work, where appropriate;
- assessing one's own oral performance through task fulfilment;
- commenting on learning issues at the end of a unit test.

It may be an unrealistic expectation for some pupils to engage in activities such as using checklists or indexing grammar points. However, teachers who build time for the development of such strategies into their lesson planning may find that this use of time is more productive than the strategy of continually moving on to new material.

2. Language-specific strategies

The teacher has a major part to play in guiding young learners to effective and convenient ways to learn. She can offer opportunities for pupils to develop their skills of prediction, analysis, inferencing, reference, memorisation.

Using cognates

It is not immediately evident to many pupils that cognates (words with the same derivation) exist. Some training is needed before full use can be made of the similarities between languages. Tasks can be set to encourage the creative use and understanding of cognates at each level of the scheme of work, this being an example based on a text from *Italia Oggi* in the late 1980s, used at Key Stage 4 (see Figure 5.2).

(i) Study the first paragraph of this text in Italian. What do you think the following words mean:

una popolazione   _____

una densità   _____

il movimento   _____

un aspetto   _____

POPOLAZIONE

L'Italia ha una popolazione di circa 56.566.000 abitanti (censimento 1981), con una densità di 187 abitanti per chilometro quadrato. Un aspetto che ha sempre influito sull'incremento demografico del Paese è il movimento emigratorio verso l'estero.

Agli inizi del nostro secolo (1900-1910), questo fenomeno — con un'uscita media di 600.000 individui l'anno — ha assunto caratteri di vero e proprio esodo. In questi ultimi tempi, però, esso sembra essersi stabilito su livelli assai più modesti, intorno, cioé, a 120.000 persone all'anno; calcolo, comunque, piuttosto approssimativo per via della libera circolazione esistente fra i Paesi della Comunità Economica Europea, per cui è assai difficile dare un'esatta dimensione del fenomeno.

A tale riguardo, va sottolineato che agli inizi del secolo le correnti emigratorie si dirigevano per lo più verso Paesi d'oltremare, mentre dal secondo dopoguerra esse fluiscono verso le altre Nazioni europee.

Nonostante il movimento emigratorio nel primo settantennio (1861-1931), la popolazione italiana è pressocché raddoppiata, mentre nel successivo cinquantennio (1931-1981) la popolazione è aumentata del 36%.

Anni	Popolazione residente	Popolazione presente	Superficie territoriale	Densità ab./km quadrato
1861	22.182.000	21.777.334	248.032	89
1931	41.651.617	41.176.671	310.079	134
1961	50.623.569	49.903.378	301.224	168
1971	54.136.547	53.770.371	301.243	180
1981	56.556.911	56.336.185	301.268	187

Figure 5.2

(ii) List any other words that you think you can identify in the first paragraph.

(iii) From the evidence of the first paragraph, predict the Italian form for the following words:

manipulation   _____

multiplication   _____

quality   _____

quantity   _____

society   _____

(iv) The word *aspetto* = aspect. We often find that English 'ct' or 'pt' changes to 'tt' in Italian. A number of relationships exist like this and they can help us to guess meaning.

Guess the meanings of:

rispetto	*un fatto*
contatto	*un contratto*
perfetto	*un concetto*

Now, look at the following groups of words and work out what they mean.

la creazione	*la nazione*	*la rivoluzione*		
responsabile	*incredibile*	*possibile*		
la televisione	*una decisione*	*una riunione*		
decorare	*celebrare*	*creare*	*meditare*	*esitare*
abolire	*demolire*	*finire*	*punire*	*brandire*

Can you devise any explanations for the patterns you see in these groups?

(v) Look through the second paragraph and find the Italian for:

this phenomenon   _____

120,000 people per annum   _____

it is very difficult   _____

Can you find any other cognates in this text? And can you suggest any more patterns?

The level of the class may be such that instructions can be put in the target language. Here, the key objective is to develop positive use of translation to promote an appreciation of cognate relationships.

Encouraging reference skills

At Key Stage 3, learners will need an introduction to the conventions of a dictionary with frequent and authentic use to consolidate. Horsfall (1997) provides a brief, but useful discussion about the teaching of dictionary skills at secondary level. As a minimum, pupils need to be taught how a dictionary is organised and how it works, what each entry contains (definitions of different meanings, examples of use, grammar, etc.), the abbreviations used in the dictionary. A range of Collins publications (Alder 1997, Pillette 1997) offer useful guidance for busy teachers on the teaching of bilingual dictionary skills and for developing dictionary skills in German, Spanish and French. At regular intervals in Key Stage 4 and possibly beyond, these skills will need further development (whether or not dictionaries are allowed in examinations):

(i) *Cherchez les mots soulignés dans le dictionnaire. Qu'est-ce que vous apprenez dans le dictionnaire?*

Pierre avait besoin d'un pull rouge pour une représentation qu'il allait faire au lycée. Il a ouvert la commode *et a trouvé un pull rouge, tour de poitrine 96, trop petit pour lui. Donc, il a remis le pull dans* le tiroir. *Malheureusement, il a dû aller aux Nouvelles Galeries pour acheter un pull, tour de poitrine 102. Après avoir payé à la* caisse, *il a vite couru à l'arrêt d'autobus.*

Quelles leçons à propos de l'utilisation du dictionnaire avec-vous apprises des mots que vous avez cherchées?

(ii) Maintenant, trouvez le français pour:

a shopping basket   soap
a wastepaper basket   a soap opera

It is important to develop dictionary skills in pupils as early as possible, starting perhaps with a lesson early in secondary education on how to use (and not mis-use!) the word list at the back of a textbook.

Learning idioms (Key Stage 4 and sixth form)

Able students can be challenged to 'collect' idioms for use in their own speech and writing, when and where they would be appropriate. Idioms are picturesque ways of saying things and they cannot be translated word for word. Simple tasks can be set, for example:

Can you work out the meanings of these expressions? Use a dictionary when required.

(i)   *Il a un grain dans la tête.*
(ii)   *Elle a fait la sourde oreille.*
(iii)   *Il a la langue bien pendue.*

Now, use a Collins Robert dictionary to find:

(i)   Lend me a hand, please.
(ii)   They got on like a house on fire.

Students can be advised that it is a good idea to note down and 'save' idioms in a special section of a notebook/file. Their idiom bank will help them to acquire some unusual and impressive language.

Private reading and listening

Many learners benefit from the opportunity to work silently on the language, sifting and processing the input. Adequate time and space needs to be given to reading (and listening) that does not involve the stress of having to produce language, with resources openly accessible. Reading materials, available from a wide variety of sources for all levels, include, among many others:

- coursebook-related CD-ROMS, newspapers on CD-ROM, foreign language reference works, for example encyclopaedias;
- published reading packages for Key Stage 3, for instance, *Vu et lu* (Colley 1996) and *Néothèque* (Hewer 1995), *Maxilire* (Bourdais *et al.*); for Key Stage 4 readers are also available, sometimes related to established coursebooks, for example *Bouquins à la Mode* (Finnie *et al.* 1998, related to the themes of Sprake *et al.*'s *Francoscope à la Mode* (1997));
- authentic materials for Key Stage 4 and A Level students, for example, Authentik Language Learning Resources Ltd.

Also available to many schools through the World Wide Web are reading materials and language games. The British Educational Communications Technology Agency (BECTa) provides regularly up-dated information on the possibilities. The facility for supplementary study on a self-access basis (lunch-times, free study periods) is being increasingly exploited. The National Grid for Learning provides further opportunities for access to materials that support the learning of foreign languages (see Chapter 11 for guidance on the use of ICT in modern languages teaching).

While recognising the limitations associated with reading schemes, we would advocate an eclectic approach to reading, with departments offering classes opportunities for a balanced diet of readers, brochures, authentic texts, magazines, CD-ROM/Internet material and newspapers. Reading practice can also be offered with single texts that focus on recently practised language, for example at Key Stage 4:

Ma Vie en France

Je m'appelle Christine Palar et j'habite à Carcassonne avec mes trois enfants. Mais, je ne suis pas française. Je suis née à Sept-Iles au Québec, donc je suis canadienne. Je suis venue en France le 15 octobre 1985. Je n'avais pas l'intention de rester en France mais j'ai trouvé du travail dans une agence de publicité. C'etait bien payé et très intéressant. Maintenant, je suis directrice de ventes.

Mon mari est canadien aussi. Il n'etait pas très heureux quand je lui ai dit que je n'allais pas retourner au Québec. Il a decidé de rester au Canada. Mes parents y habitent aussi.

Nos enfants sont nés en France. Malheureusement, ils ont des problèmes avec la langue anglaise. Moi, je suis trilingue (français, anglais et espagnol) et mon mari parle assez bien l'anglais mais à la maison nous avons toujours parlé français.

Naturellement, les enfants n'ont pas l'habitude de parler anglais et ils n'aiment pas l'étudier au collège. C'est dommâge parce que nous avons visité le Canada trois fois depuis leur naissance et ça a été un peu difficile pour les enfants.

J'adore la France surtout le Sud. Je me sens chez moi et je ne voudrais pas vivre au Canada maintenant. Je pense que les enfants préfèrent le soleil et la nourriture ici en France. Le climat est formidable et on peut faire les sports de neige comme au Canada. Naturellement, mes parents me manquent quelquefois mais j'ai beaucoup d'amis.

Nom _____ *Prénom* _____

Nationalité _____ *Profession* _____

Situation de famille _____

Date d'arrivée en France _____

Ville _____

Connaissance de langues _____

Avantages de la vie en France _____

_____

Désavantages _____

This type of activity provides opportunities for silent analysis at a personal as opposed to teacher-directed pace. A selection of texts can be laid out in library mode for learners to process in pairs. To accompany the above text, you might have a pen-friend letter about daily life, a diary extract, an account of a day in the life of a disabled person. Published material is available to support reading development to GCSE level, for example, Buckby and Corney's *Réussir à Lire* (1998).

If you need to develop quicker reading among your learners, you might look for advice to Buzan (1997) who shows how readers can be encouraged to digest rapidly large amounts of reading material. This is particularly relevant to the use of Internet materials and to sixth form work.

Prediction

An initial pre-reading or pre-listening activity could be prediction of the content of the different texts, with pairs of pupils speculating from the titles of extracts. Prediction activities prepare pupils for the finding of meaning, for interaction with the text.

Predictions can also be elicited from accompanying visuals, diagrams, and headlines, in the form of questions to be answered as one goes through the text. Such activities encourage a skill that has application across the curriculum.

Listening poses greater difficulties but school departments have gradually built up cassette resources that can be lent out for homework or supplementary study. Teachers should beware of overusing the cassette recorder. Their own input in the early years is possibly more valuable, given that in real life voices are attached to bodies that are usually close by, thus making spoken language much more accessible and comprehensible. Effective use of the cassette recorder from Year 7 will be improved if this is kept in mind.

Fortunate departments have been able to use assistants to create 'authentic' listening texts to be multi-copied for loan to students at home. This approach is particularly useful in Years 12–13 where radio and TV broadcasts are a good source of authentic material. Indeed, in some sixth form classes where numbers are small, self-access work with video recordings is regularly offered.

If a department can build up a store of cassettes of popular foreign language music these can be loaned to motivated students in the same way as library books. Where assistants are available, they may be prepared to transcribe the words to songs so that students have the support of the transcript as they listen.

Some learners benefit from hearing the text as they read. Again, if possible, an assistant could record some of the class readers for loan to pupils when they take the book. With headphones, they can listen even during class activities provided that enough machines and headphones are available.

While recognising the considerable effort and time involved in creating these learning opportunities, we believe that departmental plans can accommodate one or two new initiatives per year and so build resources gradually. Otherwise, it is hard to see how we can accommodate varied learning styles and promote greater learner autonomy. Such developments would also reduce classroom stress because they give welcome and necessary relief from the oral activities that have come to dominate.

Developing communication strategies

Learners need to be able to develop skills in working out the meaning of text, both spoken and written and in explaining things.

Qu'est-ce qu'on cherche? Ecoutez la conversation et identifiez l'objet décrit. Remplissez les cases suivantes:

Magasin	Objet Décrit
1.	
2.	

1. *Bonjour, je peux vous aider?*
    Ah, oui, je voudrais acheter quelque chose pour ouvrir les bouteilles.
    Quelles bouteilles, madame?
    Des bouteilles de vin. Je ne sais pas comment ça se dit en français.
    Ah, madame, vous cherchez un tire-bouchon. C'est ça, n'est-ce pas?

2. *Bonjour, madame. J'ai besoin de quelque chose pour réparer mon vélo.*
    Qu'est-ce qu'il y a, mademoiselle?
    J'ai un pneu crevé. Je cherche des trucs en caoutchouc ... hmmmmm ... plastiques ... pour couvrir le problème ... pardon ...
    Je vois, des pastilles?
    Oui, je suppose, un paquet de pastilles, s'il vous plaît.

Pupils can listen to a number of similar situations to work out the setting and the object sought. Lots of useful household objects can be used as content material: drawing pins, safety pins, a spanner, a stapler, a needle and thread. The listening can lead to an oral problem-solving activity where pupils have to use the kind of coping language (that they have isolated in study) to obtain certain vital objects for example, a tin opener, a kettle, a waste-paper basket, a watering can (for the plants in your flat?). Pictures or drawings of the objects can serve as prompts.

General tasks can be set for listening texts, for example:

- identifying the relationships between speakers (boss/worker, salesperson/client);
- classifying the moods of speakers (angry, sad, happy, sorry);
- listening to parts of text then predicting what speakers will say next;
- noting where conversations take place.

Similar activities should be encouraged for reading.

Focus on difficulties

Pinpointing and analysing known areas of difficulty can be effective in improving acquisition of correct forms, above all, in the development of writing, a much neglected but important skill. The technique should only be used occasionally otherwise it loses its impact. The task may concentrate on accuracy, for example in spelling:

Study these columns and consider the pattern in each case:

bien	eau	neuf	chevaux
tien	beau	deux	animaux
chien	peau	bleu	travaux
mien	couteau	neveu	journaux
lien	chateau	cheveux	canaux

Remplissez les blancs avec un des mots ci-dessus:

Carcassonne, le 8 juin

Chère Céline,

J'espère que ça va _____ chez toi.
Moi, je suis en vacances et le _____ temps est
arrivé. Donc, j'ai eu la chance de passer un peu de
temps avec mes _____. Hier soir, je me suis
promenée dans la forêt avec mon _____ qui
s'appelle Rex. Comme tu sais, j'ai _____ lapins
aussi. Ils s'appellent Bob et Jules.

Je voudrais bien faire du cheval, mais
ça coûte très cher. J'adore les _____. Il y a un
club de cheval près de chez moi, mais ça coûte très
cher, _____ cents francs (900 F) par mois.

Et toi, qu'est-ce que tu fais ces jours-ci?
Au revoir.

_____
_____

Figure 5.3

At Key Stage 4, if this technique can be applied to a piece of authentic text, for example a newspaper extract with keywords blanked, then so much the better. At Key Stage 3, it may be more difficult to find authentic and simple texts that are appropriate to learner needs.

Another fruitful area is grammar or style enhancement at Key Stage 4 or Years 12–13:

Remplissez les blancs avec un des mots ou phrases ci-dessous:

surtout	*malgré*	*d'abord*	*pourtant*	*par conséquent*
malheureusement	*pendant que*	*mais*	*donc*	

> *Chez moi, le 12 mars*
>
> *Salut Fabienne,*
>
> *Je t'ai cherchée samedi dernier. _____*
> *tu n'étais pas chez toi.*
>
> *_____, je suis allée toute seule à la côte. Il*
> *faisait très mauvais. _____ la pluie et le vent, je me*
> *suis promenée sur la plage. _____ _____ je grimpais*
> *sur un rocher je suis tombée, ce n'est pas grave _____*
> *je me suis coupé le bras. _____ _____, j'ai décidé de*
> *rentrer. En route, j'ai rencontré ton copain, Christophe. Il voudrait*
> *te voir. Est-ce que tu peux lui téléphoner?*

Figure 5.4

None of these strategies is new and the willingness to consult and involve learners is not new, but the investigation of how each person can best learn helps teachers to make teaching more effective.

Interactive strategies

Pair work

Pair activities are safer and easier to organise than group tasks. There is often a dynamic for them in that many pupils help one another, reviewing together, correcting and testing each other. Teacher-organised tasks may range from simple mechanical practice of a dialogue to an information gap activity involving some freedom of choice. Cue cards tend to be popular because they allow pupils to practise without teacher domination. Examples of these abound in textbooks and useful exploitable practice books that allow for confidence-building repetition (see Bibliography). They give learners time to focus on one restricted area of language, but have disadvantages if overused. Card games can also be useful, particularly with younger learners, many of whom enjoy having something to touch and hold as they practise. Again, such practice allows for repetition, though with careful preparation it can be developed into a more challenging and meaningful activity.

Find out what your partner thinks. Turn a card (see Figure 5.5) and ask your partner:

'Que penses-tu de ça?'

Figure 5.5

Results can be recorded if desired (Figure 5.6) and the activity can be done in small groups of three or four.

Nom	nager	tricoter	chanter	jouer avec un ordinateur	danser

Figure 5.6

The preparation for such cards is time-consuming but once done the cards can be used for a variety of verb forms and tenses:

Qu'est-ce que tu vas faire ce weekend?
Qu'est-ce que tu as fait le weekend dernier?
Est-ce que tu veux ...?
Est-ce que tu sais ...?

For vocabulary and pattern practice, handling of real objects, packets, boxes, bottles and small toys helps to reinforce meaning during practice. Teachers with small children are at an advantage here, often able to assist practice with toy buses, trains, boats, taxis, bikes. One of the most popular activities we have used with low attainers is the matching of toy farm and zoo animals to labels on plans of farms and zoos.

Town maps offer opportunities for work on directions or prepositions such as 'near', 'opposite', 'in front of'. At Key Stage 3, they can be very simple. You each have a town map but with different information. In the following example, pupils always start at the station. They have to find the way to the places listed and mark them on their map, without showing the map to their partner.

Pupil A	*Pupil B*
De la gare, tu dois aller –	*De la gare, tu dois aller –*
au stade	*à l'Hotel du Nord*
à la poste	*au commissariat*
à l'hôpital	*à la piscine*

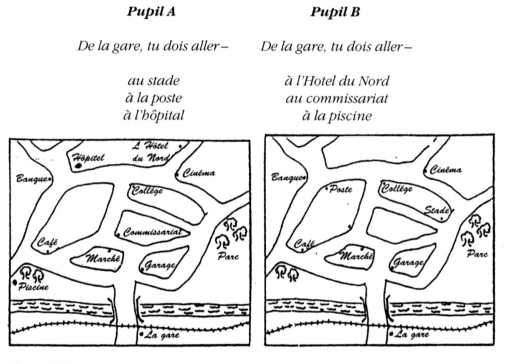

Figure 5.7

Traditional exercises can be transformed into information gap activities for a pair of students. Consider this example adapted from an exercise of Pincas (1982, p. 1), for an individual to practise reading and writing, or for a pair to practise asking and answering questions.

Complète les renseignements dans la carte d'identité. Ton partenaire a les informations nécessaires.

Remplis les blancs dans les phrases suivantes. Ton partenaire a les informations nécessaires.

CARTE D'IDENTITE

Nom ... Cartier ....

Prénom ....

Age .... Date de naissance 21.03.63 ....

Lieu de naissance Perpignan ....

Taille ....

Yeux ...... Cheveux .... marron ....

Signes particuliers ....

Situation de famille ....

Profession ....

Figure 5.8

Description de Miriam

Miriam . . . est ouvrière dans une imprimerie. Elle est née le . . . à . . . dans le Sud de la France. Elle a . . . ans.

Son mari est né dans le nord de la Belgique. Elle a deux enfants qui s'appellent Fabienne et Luc.

Miriam a les cheveux courts et . . . Elle a les . . . verts. A cause d'un accident, elle a une cicatrice au menton. Elle mesure un mètre soixante-cinq.

For greater authenticity, the description could be in the body of a letter, for instance, from someone answering a request for a pen-friend exchange.

All the above strategies take time to prepare. To avoid unreasonable and excessive amounts of time spent in preparation, it is as well to think of how one can insert quick pairs practice into the general development of normal 'bread and butter' lessons, based on existing resources such as the textbook or OHP. Consider where pupils might benefit from working together for a short time and you may find that you already have the material to hand for pair work activities.

Group work

This is more difficult to manage and sustain, but once established it can be of enormous benefit. For younger learners it is essential that the task be clear and guided.

Using pictures

Matching and recall activities can be done in groups, for example matching labels to pictures and taking the labels away to see if the language can be recalled.

At Key Stage 4 some schools still use picture stories, a useful narrative device. With careful presentation and preparation, this can lead to groups matching strips of text to pictures, reading the text, then withdrawing strips of text to see if they can recall and re-tell the story from just a few prompts. A system of turns needs to be clearly established and followed if the technique is to succeed. Pupils always have the strips of text available should they get 'stuck' so that they can prompt one another.

1	2
Il y a deux jours je suis sortie avec mon amie Sonia.	*Un petit enfant jouait au bord du lac . . .*

3	4
Soudain, l'enfant a couru . . .	

Find your partner

This activity is done with the whole group and can take many forms. Its success largely depends on the maturity of the group. Is it responsible enough to move around in a safe and purposeful manner to complete the task in the target language?

Each pupil is given a new identity which he must keep secret. The teacher asks them to find someone with the same name, age and town. She may throw in a couple of groups of three just to make the task a little longer. Each person has a card like Figure 5.9.

There is plenty of opportunity for practice in a purposeful context. The activity can be exploited for all areas of experience in modern courses, for example, find someone going on the same holiday as you at the same time; someone who shares the same interests as you; someone who has similar ambitions to you.

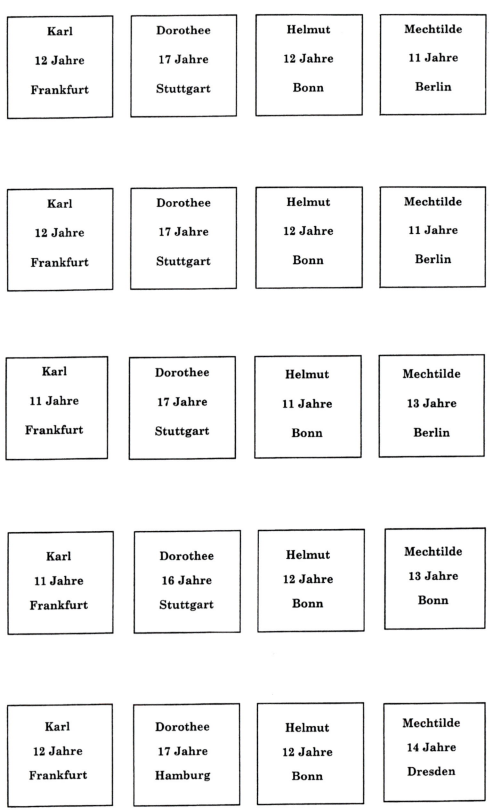

Figure 5.9

Find someone who . . .

In this variation, pupils circulate and use yes/no questions in Italian:

Trova qualcuno che	nome
gioca ál tennis	_____
ha due fratelli	_____
lavora il weekend	_____
sa guidare	_____
parla Panjabi	_____

Figure 5.10

Dice and board games

These can be devised very quickly from available materials. In Figure 5.11 all that is needed is a dice, paper and pencils. The game is played in groups of four with each player making up an identity for him or herself. At the throw of the dice the player asks a question of another member of the group, according to the number thrown. If he or she has filled the three spaces in that category, then a turn is missed. The first person to complete the grid with correct information is the winner.

1	Nome	Silvia
2	Età	40
3	Data di Nascita	06.07.53
4	Nazionalità	Canadese
5	Stato Civile	Sposata
6	Professione	Giudice

Figure 5.11

An element of chance is introduced and, provided that pupils keep their identities secret, there is a valid information gap. The same format can be used in the areas of leisure, daily routine, family, jobs, salary and ambitions. For the activity to work effectively, there needs to have been adequate controlled practice of the question forms so that pupils have some familiarity with question formation.

Further examples of interactive tasks can be found in Chapters 3, 4 and 7. They provide a time and place for the practice of a limited amount of language in a supportive and success-oriented framework. Feelings of success have been shown to be one of the most motivating factors in language learning. If practice gives such feelings, it is likely that learners will be more willing to engage in practice tasks.

Problem solving

Giving pairs or groups tasks to work on and resolve using resources available can be useful in the promotion of confidence and autonomy. Different levels of support can be given to suit the needs of individual groups. This example was written by a Working Party of Tameside teachers:

Alltagliche Probleme – *wie kann man sie lösen?*

Benutze:

Man muss
ich rate dir/Ihnen, . . . zu
vergiss/vergessen Sie nicht, dass . . .
man soll
geh/gehen Sie!
man muss/du musst/Sie müssen
man kann/du kannst/Sie können
versuch/versuchen Sie

1. *Du hast den Bus in die Stadtmitte verpasst. Du hast es eilig.*

2. *Sie wollen ein Omelett kochen, aber die Eier sind alle.*

3. *Man muss eine Tasse Kaffee machen aber ohne Gas und Elektrizität.*

4. *Du hast Hunger. Du willst etwas zum Essen kaufen, hast aber kein Geld.*

Group oral assignments

Tasks can be set for groups of three or four students to engage in a review of their progress. They perform the task then discuss how well they think they were able to perform in the group for example,

1. Give a one-minute talk about your likes/dislikes/hobbies.
2. Ask a partner:
   a) what she likes doing at the weekend;
   b) what her favourite hobby is;
   c) what she is going to do tonight.
3. Describe the picture in the envelope to your partners who should try to draw it.
4. Interview your partners about their likes/dislikes (see Figure 5.12):

Nom	Passetemps préféré	la télévision	le cinéma	le judo

Figure 5.12

Each pupil is given a different set of tasks and asked to prepare them before beginning the group activity. Members of the group perform the tasks cooperatively, interacting and supporting one another when communication breaks down. Then when the tasks are complete they review and assess their performance.

While the activities suggested are well-known and largely teacher-directed, they provide opportunities for learners to engage in practice, cooperative working, mutual support and exploration of the language. Furthermore, when the purpose of the activities is made clear, pupils may begin to arrive at a greater awareness of the nature of language learning.

We have not attempted here to provide a coherent progressive programme of learner training that can be integrated into schemes of work, just some suggestions for classroom use. With opportunities for negotiation in schools, teachers and pupils can see one another as partners in learning. This emphasis brings more autonomy and effectiveness to learning, as learners gradually become more self-aware and independent. We believe that the development of learner independence is a gradual process that cannot be achieved through a crash programme of learner training, but by a regular infusion of opportunities for practice and exploration.

Clearly, we have only provided a sample of the possibilities, so in the later sections of this book we make suggestions that we feel may make learning more effective, particularly in the areas of vocabulary and grammar.

Section 3: The target language

Chapter 6

Using the target language

Experts are often dogmatic about the topic of using the target language in the classroom. The prevailing ideal seems to be that teachers should move towards the almost total use of the target language while they are with their pupils. The example of teachers of English as a foreign language (TEFL) is often cited. TEFL textbooks and lessons are usually totally in English, no matter what the audience. The analogy is, however, not a fair one. It is more realistic to make comparisons with the teaching of French in Germany, the teaching of English in Italian state schools or the teaching of Spanish in Denmark. In these cases, language teachers from the UK will find many areas of comparison. Teaching languages in the state education system cannot easily be compared to private language-school settings in which English is taught to learners from overseas.

We feel that this is a sensitive aspect of methodology and that it is unwise to be dogmatic. The teaching aims on which this chapter are based are to:

- be realistic about the use of the target language;
- identify ways of maximising the use of the target language;
- encourage teachers to overcome their own sense of guilt about the use of English;
- bear in mind that teaching is about the art of the possible;
- remember that denial of the mother tongue can be demoralising.

This chapter attempts to make a number of practical suggestions, but the wise teacher will tailor them to suit his or her own needs. As in other areas of methodology, it is not always possible to adopt wholesale approaches which have worked for other people in teaching situations other than one's own.

Language teachers aim to enable their pupils to be confident in using the language they are learning. In the process of attempting this they encounter a number of problems, each of which requires a range of strategies to solve it.

Using English in language lessons

Many language teachers carry a burden of guilt concerning the amount of English they use, especially with more challenging classes. Switching codes, from target language to English and back, is a frequent occurrence in languages lessons. It has been frowned upon but has not been eradicated. It merits further study before it is dismissed, so that teachers can see how and when it is most effective. While acknowledging concerns about target language use, for example at Key Stage 4 (Dobson 1998), we share the view that methodology cannot ignore the role of the mother tongue in second language learning (Cook 1996) or seek to isolate it. And, there are instances when it is inevitable, even advisable to use English.

In the following sections, such instances will be highlighted, though you must bear in mind that learning a language involves as much exposure to it and use of it as possible. Teachers should maximise their own and, more importantly, their pupils' use of the target language. The amount of target language pupils can use or tolerate depends on such factors as their ability and motivation. The teacher has to be sensitive to this and react accordingly. Most pupils can cope with, at the most, ten minutes immersion in the target language without losing concentration. In the early stages of learning, demand for a lot of production of target language can be daunting for pupils. A minority can cope with longer stretches.

Dealing with errors

The language classroom is a place where teachers hope that pupils will take risks with words and structures, try things out. They will only do this if they consider that their classroom is a safe place in which their self-esteem will not be damaged by over-correction. If a pupil is corrected each time she says or writes a word, she will play for safety and avoid experimentation. The natural and traditional impulse of a foreign language teacher is to correct the pupils whenever they make an error in their spoken target language. This becomes an even stronger reflex action if the teacher is involved with the pupils' written work in the target language. This impulse is a sign of the caring teacher, not of a negative one. Teachers want their pupils to 'get it right'. Nevertheless this impulse can be counter-productive. Pupils who expect that their teacher will correct them every time they open their mouths or put pen to paper tend to become reluctant to do either for fear of retribution or public embarrassment. Fluency work, in which the pupil is encouraged to use target language for sustained periods without fear of being corrected, will most likely increase the pupils' confidence and result in their taking language 'risks'. One can, after all, only learn by trying and making mistakes. Otherwise nobody would ever experiment.

Implications for the classroom

1. Identify the times when you are going to concentrate on accuracy and tell the pupils what you are doing. It may be best done when you are in front of the class, but you can set up group and pair activities which focus on accuracy, for example paired dictation exercises. After some years of disgrace, dictation

is proving a versatile tool to develop accuracy (see, for example, Davis and Rinvolucri 1988, Wajnryb 1990). For oral accuracy you or a pupil can 'become' a computer which responds only to completely accurate target language.

2. Correct pronunciation errors only if they are recurrent and interfere with understanding. Model rather than correct. In other words, use the correct form in your response to the pupils, without emphasising anything to show you have noted an error.

3. When pupils are engaged in tasks, correct only at controlled stages of the lesson.

4. Correct written work using the target language if it is possible. *Bien!* or *Prima!* are encouraging comments, but a more extensive written indication of strengths or weaknesses every now and then may have to be in English to facilitate understanding.

5. At Key Stage 3 detailed correction of written work should include the correction of copied material, for incorrect copying is the source of many errors in writing.

6. Mark written work selectively. Select particular aspects to concentrate on and tell the pupils what you are doing. Marking every word should not be a habitual practice.

7. Much depends on the ability of the pupil. Abler children may be able to cope with more correction; but do not depend on it. Even able pupils thrive on the experience of success and need reassurance.

8. It is advisable to provide an occasional written comment on pupils' oral work, so that they have a permanent written record of their oral progress.

The pupils' need to understand

If the teacher uses the target language for an extensive amount of time, there is a possibility that a number of pupils will be left behind, particularly underachievers, pupils with learning difficulties, those who think they have lost before they begin to try, pupils with attention-span problems. The use of the target language should be supported by visual cues, gesture, mime and frequent comprehension checks. Nevertheless the use of English to assist understanding should still be part of the agenda, if it cannot be avoided.

Implications for the classroom

To assist comprehension you can:

- 'model' activities yourself;
- give examples of what you mean as they are much easier to take in than the simplest of explanations;
- use your own cues to assist meaning: pictures, flashcards, signals, mime, gestures. Even use English alongside the target language as an initial cue. Analyse your cues to see which ones permit the pupils to dispense with the need to listen to the target language and which ones are natural to the way you normally communicate. Try to withdraw gradually those cues which

replace the target language, particularly the gestures, so long as you do not lose the class;
- train your pupils to ignore redundant language and to extract meaning;
- select class 'interpreters' to explain what you are saying. The formality of calling them interpreters avoids the possible irritation which can be caused by repeatedly asking for translations;
- use English when necessary as a short cut to reduce pupil frustration.

To check understanding regularly you can:

- do a regular face-scan around the class, especially pupils' eyes (pretending to listen);
- do a regular class-scan to detect 'twitches', restlessness;
- provide yourself with feedback by checking things out orally or in writing;
- teach the pupils appropriate forms of interruption if they do not follow, but make the rules of how and when to interrupt quite clear.

The least able, whether they are in mixed-ability groups or not, can only take in brief instructions or one instruction at a time. As a result they need support in the following ways:

- from you, if you are able to give them the time in the full class context, using English or, if possible, target language as you move about the room;
- from the rest of the class, if you are able to establish a relationship with them which will enable them to think that it is natural to be supportive to other pupils;
- from group and/or pair work, in which the peers will be able to help in ways which are sometimes more pupil-friendly than the approach of the teacher. Children tend to be good-natured in these circumstances and benefit from the relationships involved, from the opportunity to develop leadership and other social skills and from the benefits to their own learning when they explain to someone else or help them;
- from visual props, such as worksheets which accompany your explanation or word flashcards. By placing word flashcards in a conspicuous place (use masking tape; it is not messy), you are able to help those pupils who take in information better through their eyes than through their ears, when you are teaching new or unfamiliar words or phrases. They act as a reference point which is always there during the teaching of a unit and will help avoid the mispronunciations which arise when pupils see the spelling of a word some time after they hear it spoken for the first time. As you introduce the language, you can actually point out the connections between the spoken and written word;
- from special needs support staff, if your school actually deploys them in classrooms rather than in a withdrawal system. It should be noted that to withdraw pupils from some or all foreign language lessons could be considered by many to be a denial of pupils' rights of access to the full curriculum and therefore a denial of equality of opportunity.

Classroom organisation

It is difficult to get on with a lesson before you have organised the class to carry out the task you are setting. This can be a problem if you wish to use the target language to do so.

The following all present challenges to the uninterrupted flow of the target language:

- introducing a new topic, when it has to be clear in order to support the pupils' motivation;
- explaining the rules of a new game, when chaos can ensue when the rules are misunderstood;
- giving grammatical explanations, when the abstract material entails complex concepts;
- setting homework, especially in a mixed-ability class.

Implications for the classroom

1. Teach the pupils how to listen. Use listening games which practise and test the language which will come into play in classroom organisation:

   (a) A version of 'Simon says' (useful and popular in Key Stages 2 and 3) will quickly run through many of the instructions you wish to practise. Pupils can take the teacher's role in this to increase the fun.
   (b) Give a series of ten instructions one after the other. Pupils work in groups to recall them without writing anything down. Each group must then carry out the instructions. The teacher then distributes a list with the correct instructions with which the pupils can score their attempt.
   (c) Walking dictation is a game which draws on all four skills. It is based on having a copy of a text on each wall of the room. Pupils sit in groups and each group send one envoy at a time to read, remember and then return to dictate what they recall of the text. The first group to have a perfect copy has won.
   (d) Where the pupils have a series of instructions to follow in order to perform a task or complete a piece of work, put the target language instructions on the board in muddled order and ask pupils to put them in the correct order.

2. When you set homework, try to give the pupils a visual as well as an aural instruction. Write it on the board, for example. If you say it in English to make sure they understand, print it in the target language on the board. Plan sufficient time for this activity and avoid the rush in the last three minutes of the lesson, when many pupils will either copy down incorrectly or miss the whole thing.

3. Use the target language as far as possible when you first introduce a new topic. The detailed information which follows the introduction may have to be given, at least in part, in English.

4. When explaining a new game, use mime, gesture, drawings. The class should know your personal codes, whether mimed, drawn or spoken. We all have

our shortcuts. Do the game yourself the first time, if possible. Use English to explain the first time, if it is a complicated game. The second time it is played, if you think the class will cope, use the target language. A volunteer/volunteers demonstrate. A 'mock-up' helps where appropriate.

5. It can be dangerous to decide on a list of words which must be part of a pupils' learning programme. Different client groups have different needs. Lists tend to limit rather than allow for flexibility. Nevertheless, certain words and phrases can be specified as useful. Productive language which should be taught could include the target language for:

I've forgotten . . .	*J'ai oublié . . .*
May I have a . . .?	*Puis-je avoir . . .?*
I don't know	*Je ne sais pas*
I can do it	*Je sais le faire*
I know what to do	*Je sais ce qu'il faut faire*
I don't know what to do	*Je ne sais pas ce qu'il faut faire*
I have done it	*Je l'ai fait*
I don't understand	*Je ne comprends pas/Je n'ai pas compris*
Yes/no	*Oui/non*
Come and help me, please?	*Est-ce que vous pouvez m'aider, svp?*
How do I say . . .?	*Comment dit-on . . .?*
How do you do it	*Comment ça se fait?*
That's great, brilliant, etc.	*C'est génial*
That's difficult	*C'est difficile*
That's interesting	*C'est intéressant*
What is it in French?	*C'est quoi en français?*

Receptive language which should be taught could include the vocabulary for classroom nouns and phrases for comments on written work, such as excellent, untidy, but also some of the following:

That's enough	*Ça suffit*
Pay attention!	*Fais/Faites attention!*
That will do	*Ça ira*
Translate that into French, English	*Traduis/Traduisez ça en français/anglais*
Open . . ./close . . .	*Ouvrez . . ./Fermez . . .*
Do this	*Fais ça/ Faites cela*
Copy this down	*Copiez ça*
Write this	*Ecrivez ça*
Get into groups of four	*Mettez-vous en groupes de quatre . . .*
Work with a partner	*Travaille/Travaillez avec un partenaire*
Listen	*Ecoutez*
Repeat this	*Répétez . . .*
Have you finished?	*Est-ce que tu as fini/vous avez fini?*
Have you done the exercise?	*Est-ce que tu as fait/fini l'exercice?*

You may have noticed that we omit 'What is it?' and 'What is that?' Unless you genuinely do not know what something is, '*Qu'est-ce que c'est?*' is an inept question to put to a pupil who knows that both you and she already know the answer.

6. If knowledge about grammar is taught formally, there seem to be few alternatives to the use of English at least in the earlier stages (see Chapter 7). The use of the grammatical point can be introduced in the target language and practice organised. For abler pupils it may be possible to explain a limited number of grammatical points in the target language, for example gender and the article in French, the formation of the future tense in French.

Relationships

Nothing can be more disconcerting to the teacher and to the rest of the class than the sudden interruption to the flow of activity in the target language by a pupil just bursting to tell the teacher that 'We went to France in the holidays' or 'My Mum has had a baby.' The fact that a pupil feels able to personalise his or her relationship with the teacher is a source of strength. Poor relationships between pupils and teachers do not make the normal teaching and learning environments any easier for the participants to cope with. We want to maximise the amount of target language used: a paradox! If we accept that praise is a vital form of recognition of pupil achievement, teachers may fear that it will be difficult to recognise it in the target language. This fear is unfounded. If the teacher injects the appropriate amount of emotional energy and body language into a well-merited *Très bien!*, their pupils will understand that genuine praise is being given.

Implications for the classroom

1. Get the pupils to agree to try not to interrupt the flow of the target language.
2. Agree special times for news/gossip/discussions:

   - at the end of the lesson
   - during 'time out' in the middle of a long or double lesson
   - during a whole lesson which you decide to use as a non-languages lesson, in order to give the pupils an occasional break.

3. Use the target language for praise, expression of opinions, attitudes if possible. Use, for example, the target language for:

Well done!
You speak (German/French) well!
Well said!
Well done!
Good!
Excellent!
Good work!
I like that!
I don't like that!
I am interested.

4. Use the target language for important messages where possible, that is, where you are confident that the message will be understood and acted upon. For example: '*Le bus pour la piscine partira à deux heures. Monsieur Grey vous attendra. Ne soyez pas en retard.*'

Background material

The language classroom provides the learner with much more than a foreign language. Among other experiences it offers an insight into a different way of life and moves the learner as close as she is likely to get, in many cases, to a direct experience of the culture and values of the people of another country or countries. Part of our task as teachers is to overcome ethnocentricity. There can be many instances of the teaching of background material which occur incidentally and can be taught in the target language. Modern courses and external examinations such as the GCSE presuppose cultural knowledge. For example, a role-play which expects the participants to act out getting on a German bus will take it for granted that they know about the machine which stamps tickets. *Exploring otherness* (Jones 1995) offers a wealth of ideas for how learners can experience features of another culture.

Implications for the classroom

- Lessons can sometimes be structured so that sustained amounts of background information are dealt with at a given point, for example at the end of the lesson.
- It is legitimate to teach background material in English on occasion, but where possible aspects of culture are best done in the target language.
- Try to use material from countries other than France or Spain, where the target language is spoken. Obtain letters and texts from Africa or South America. This can be done by using search engines on the Internet. The lingu@net and allnet websites both link with useful sites for French, one of which is in Africa.

Discipline, safety, class control

The use of the target language can make it much harder to control classes, to react promptly to pupils who misbehave or become distracted, to ensure that the activity that the pupils are involved in is being undertaken safely. Much depends on the receptiveness of a particular class and on the nature of that class. A very disruptive pupil in a mixed-ability class may well require a sharp reprimand in English before he or she becomes dangerous. The experience the class had the previous year with a different teacher may set the climate for at least the first few weeks as far as the use of the target language is concerned.

Implications for the classroom

- Start the process of acclimatising the pupils to the use of the target language as early as possible after they arrive at the school.
- Aim to build up a relationship with the class which will permit the use of target language for routine discipline: e.g. 'I'm waiting!' Your face and tone of voice will carry a message in themselves. In addition to phrases and expressions mentioned above, use the target language for:

Stop it!
Don't do that!
Be quiet!
Put that down!
Stop working!

- Try to use the target language, even if the pupil replies in English.
- In an extreme situation, use English. The very rarity of the event will impress on the pupils the seriousness of the situation and will become a disciplinary device.
- The whole department in a school must agree to be consistent, especially across a year group. Pupils make comparisons and will soon realise that German is 'easier' in Mr Smith's class.

Dealing with the unexpected and with interruptions

The everyday lesson is prone to a wide variety of interruptions. Schools are not predictable organisations. It is the teacher's reactions to these which really underline the status of the target language. To use English for any casual talk, for any important messages, for events in the classroom which are not part of the lesson plan is to devalue the target language. Each situation may require a different strategy. The extent to which the strategies suggested can be used depends, as usual, on the receptiveness and the ability of the class which is being taught and the range of vocabulary you have taught them to handle.

Types of interruption and how to deal with them

1. A pupil comes in with a spoken message; the teacher uses the target language and the class interprets.
2. A teacher comes in with a spoken message; the receiving teacher uses target language if she has the confidence or courage. A justification for this would be to compare it to turning on a light in a lesson in a photographic darkroom. Nevertheless, it is asking a lot of your colleagues. It would be wise to publicise your strategy in the staffroom and come to individual agreements with specific colleagues. The net result may be to decrease the number of teacher-caused interruptions to your lessons!
3. A pupil comes late to your lesson or has been absent; the pupil has to explain in the target language.
4. A pupil has not brought homework or a piece of equipment; the information and explanation should be given in the target language.

5. A window cleaner is outside or even inside the classroom; point him or her out in the target language, get back to the lesson and battle on.
6. A pupil asks a question in English; answer in the target language. You may be able to insist that she should ask the question in the target language.
7. If an accident happens, use English.

The kind of language you could draw on to deal with interruptions can include:

Teacher:
Why are you late?
Where have you been?
Whose is this?
Wait a few minutes
OK

Pupil:
I'm sorry I am late
I had to see Miss . . .
I've forgotten
I've lost it
I haven't got a . . .
May I have a . . .?
I have a message for . . .
I have a message from . . .
May I go to the toilet?

The language of assessment, recording and reporting

The issue of assessment opens a number of potential problems. It can always be relied upon to be a source of controversy in a group of teachers and has been a significant cause of concern in relation to the National Curriculum.

One problem lies in the use of target language in rubrics. It is good practice to minimise the pupils' exposure to English. Naturally, rubrics must be in the target language; otherwise the pupils will understand that 'real' information is always given in English. However, this can create a barrier between the pupil and the assessment task, so that it becomes difficult to assess her skills because she has been unable to understand what to do in the first place. Compare '*Cochez la réponse correcte*' with '*Sélectionnez la réponse que vous trouvez correcte et cochez dans la boîte.*'

If the outcome of an assessment technique is in English, the backwash effect is to minimise the use of target language in the normal lesson. This was the unforeseen outcome of the GCSE examinations in the early 1990s when many responses were in English or indeed in non-linguistic form (e.g. ticking a picture).

With regard to recording, Records of Achievement (RoAs) are undoubtedly a powerful method of motivating pupils, but target-setting and reviewing become unmanageable if one tries to carry them out in the target language. Furthermore, if processes of reviewing and recording are very time-consuming, they demotivate learners. Most would probably prefer to get on with learning rather than complete records, especially if they have to struggle with the process in the target language.

Implications for the classroom

1. If you know your class will experience difficulty, use English to explain the task, but reinforce it with the target language wherever possible, whether orally or in writing. You may be able to use the target language for the majority, but then go to individuals to explain in English or ask a pupil to 'interpret'.
2. Design assessment tasks to maximise the use of the target language (see Chapter 9).
3. Target-setting and reviewing will have to be in English for most, if not all, classes. The motivational benefits are worth the price. If the reviewing is undertaken in English, the pupil will feel at ease. Reviewing, however, is not a daily occurrence. By spacing it out, the teacher will cause fewer interruptions to the flow of target language and, of course, a fair management of her own time. By making reviews of progress a half-termly or even a termly event, the importance of the activity will be highlighted. Target-setting and reviewing will be dealt with in more detail in Chapter 9.

Other ways to maximise the use of the target language

Using a native speaker

It may be possible to bring a native speaker into the classroom, either an FLA, a colleague or a member of the local community who is prepared to come once or twice or even more frequently into the local school. Use the resource as economically as you can. It may be a luxury to expect the native speaker to work with small groups at a time. The most economical use is to bring him or her into your classroom. This must be well prepared, especially if it is a rare event. You cannot afford to have the visitor hanging around your classroom with nothing to do. Let the pupils see and hear you speaking the target language in realistic situations. Admittedly you will have to establish a good relationship with the native speaker, if you lack confidence yourself, as some teachers may do. It may be useful for the pupils to see you being corrected occasionally by her.

Another economical use of the native speaker's time is to ask her to make tape recordings or produce authentic notes, letters, postcards. To be authentic, the material should not be scripted and should be presented in scenarios. For example:

Getting repairs done

You go to a number of shops to get some repairs done. Explain what is wrong and seek advice.

1. Your camera will no longer work.
2. Your jacket/skirt has been badly stained.
3. You need to get your washing done.
4. Your shoes need mending.
5. Your glasses have been broken.

Once the material has been recorded, there is no limit to what you and the pupils can do with it. For example, with the example given, you can ask the pupils to suggest what to do with the items described. Rowles *et al.* (1997) offer a comprehensive consideration of how the work of the FLA can be organised.

Games

Language games are the closest many classrooms will get to using the target language realistically as a means to an end, rather than as an end in itself. Here are one or two examples:

(a) guessing games, for example 'I spy':

- animal, mineral, vegetable (ask questions to ascertain what the teacher/lead pupil is thinking of. He/she can only say yes or no);
- people games (guess who I am/you are). Simply think of someone or some object and pin its name on someone's back. They walk about the room asking questions to find out who/what they are.

(b) what would happen if . . . (the school disappeared, etc.)

Telephone calls

Telephone calls can be simulated in a variety of ways. Give each pupil a telephone number. This can be on a list of numbers, so that each pupil knows all the other numbers in the class, but not who they belong to, because only one number is highlighted on their own copy. They can be asked to make 'phone calls' across the classroom and experience the fun of the unexpected recipient of a call, while the rest of the class eavesdrop. Alternatively you can distribute a 'telephone directory' for the class. You may be able to acquire discarded or faulty telephone receivers to make the simulation more realistic or even use their pocket calculator to look like a mobile phone. Pupils sitting back to back with their hands to their ears as if holding a receiver have no difficulty in imagining a call. The content of the calls may be closely guided or allowing free expression, depending on the expertise of the pupils. The range of activities includes:

- pupils sit in pairs and 'ring' each other to plan a night out or some other social event;
- pupils phone around the room to find out 'news' from classmates either in real life or in simulated roles;

- pairs make an appointment to meet;
- pairs make a date;
- pairs arrange to go to a disco;
- a 'chatline' is established.

The environment

We have already discussed the use of word flashcards. There are other ways in which the learning environment can display the target language. The walls can be made to talk. Signs about the school in a number of languages serve as reminders and stress that all the places signposted have names in other languages. If you put them up, keep an eye on them so that you can act swiftly before they become worn, untidy and then ineffective.

Posters, either commercial or produced by pupils, can incorporate the target language. They can also display the results of class or individual projects.

The walls can display a wide range of images and words connected with languages being taught. You can also use the walls, if there is space, to put up *aides-memoire*, such as the numbers 1 to 100, the months of the year, the paradigm of the verb you are stressing at the moment, a chart demonstrating the use of a tense, a time-line to show the sequence of tenses used in conjoined sentences, for example, combinations of past perfect and perfect tenses in French; sentences with *depuis* (present and imperfect usages and meanings).

Multi-lingual packaging is now the norm in British shops. There has been an explosion of foreign languages in signs and packaging – department store wrappers, chocolate boxes, street signs, shop and café names. It is very easy to collect examples from every home of how foreign languages are used for commercial purposes. Pupils could be asked to bring examples to school.

Language material on walls can become wallpaper if the teacher forgets to remind pupils to refer to it as a prompt to avoid the use of English.

Monitoring

It is all too easy to agree that the task of the foreign language teacher is to maximise the use of the target language. It is equally easy to fall to the temptation to use English. It is hard to sustain target language, particularly with a difficult class or the last lesson on a Friday, when the teacher is tired or, more likely, worn out. Bad teaching habits are soon formed and it is not easy to escape from the English-speaking rut, once a class has grown comfortable with it. Some teachers lack the range of skills necessary to influence the fluency and confidence of their pupils. National curriculum pronouncements on the prime place of the target language and school departmental policy documents can only have the status of advice, implemented by common consent, not imposed by diktat. Once the classroom door is closed, teachers need to keep some check on the amount of English used in their classrooms. Ideas for doing this are given below.

Implications for the classroom

There are many ways in which target language use can be promoted and monitored.

1. Make a 'contract' with yourself to use the target language for up to ten minutes each lesson/more than ten minutes each lesson/half a lesson/one lesson per week. Self-monitoring is the best form of control.
2. Place prompts on your desk. Note down ten to twelve words or phrases in the target language which you want to make a point of using in class over the period of a few weeks and focus on three or four a week.
3. Make a 'contract' with the pupils for them to use the target language for initially five minutes, then two spurts of five minutes separated by another activity. Gradually increase the amount. Always remember to recognise at the end of a lesson the extent to which a class has met its target. A stopwatch can be used on occasion.
4. Consider using a 'fines and rewards' system (teams, points, stars) to recognise sustained use of the target language.
5. Have target language days, when your class or even the whole school has to use an identified language in all circumstances. A sign such as a French *tricolore* in the room or the school entrance can signal this happening.
6. Use the pupils to monitor your own adherence to the use of the target language. Take them into your confidence and they will not only remind you when you fall by the wayside but will also increase their own use. This makes the pupils part of the teaching process in the best sense of the words.
7. Colleagues can be invited into your classroom to observe you and give you feedback on, for example, the number of instances when you used English, yet could have naturally avoided it.
8. Negotiate with the pupils the rules for the use of English and train them to ask permission to use English when they need to.
9. The departmental scheme of work can include lists of words which should be taught to specific year groups as props for the sustained use of target language.
10. The idea of authenticity is often carried too far, almost to the point of obsession. Materials which include authentic elements are useful cultural teaching aids. Many materials which include amounts of target language may be utterly 'inauthentic', but are good fun and enjoyed by the pupils.
11. Whole-class or group assignments or projects can draw on extensive use of the target language in writing or in speech (see Chapter 9).

A substantial element of the National Curriculum documentation in the early 1990s was devoted to the use of the target language. In our opinion it is unwise, if not unrealistic, to legislate on how teachers should teach. Try as we may, we cannot impose methods on a teacher, we can only advocate them. Nevertheless it is self-evident that all language teachers strive to a greater or lesser extent to use the target language in their teaching. The greater the extent the better for teachers, pupils and the cause of language learning, so long as realism and relevance remain the guiding principles.

Chapter 7

The teaching and learning of grammar

One misconception associated with communicative approaches led to a loss of belief in grammar teaching in the classroom (Thompson 1996). Teachers sometimes found it necessary to teach grammar almost secretly, while others strenuously avoided references to grammar. Consequently, some teachers may still not be sure how and where it fits with communicative approaches, even though the teaching of grammar has been rehabilitated in the new National Curriculum for modern foreign languages. There are many English language teaching sources of ideas for teaching grammar (for example, Ur 1988, Harmer 1987, Rinvolucri 1984) and for modern languages teachers there are now a number of sources, for example, Rendall 1998, and Halliwell 1993, who reminded us that grammar does matter.

The 11–16 curriculum allows for at most 400 hours of foreign language teaching in any one language (Wringe 1989). This is hardly likely to allow time for the input required for an effective acquisition of the language in the manner of an infant learning its first language. The process is necessarily much more hurried and of course, it is a lot more foreign than first language acquisition. Classroom experience suggests to us that the teaching of grammar can and does contribute to rapid acquisition if it allows some learners to

- process new language more readily;
- understand the language more effectively;
- classify language items in ways that assist learning.

Structures and functions

If using the language in a variety of contexts is the key to rapid acquisition, pupils should have the chance to practise as much as possible. In addition, when teaching a structure, it is important to be clear about its function in the language. Therefore, we afford opportunities for our pupils not only to see and use the structure in isolation but also to fulfil one or more functions with it. Later, we encourage learners to use the structure to fulfil functions in other contexts. If they can write a letter to book a hotel room, they should have some idea of what to do when writing to a youth hostel or campsite. If they can express opinions about their preferences with regard to music, they should have some language they can appy to a discussion of other preferences, for example, films or sports. The key is that the teaching of grammar includes opportunities for language use in realistic ways.

An example of our own experience may illustrate. As eleven-year-olds at school, we were taught the 'imperative'. Dutifully, we learned it and may even have translated with it. But, it was years before we gave anyone a real instruction, or read a series of real instructions (from a recipe or telephone booth, perhaps). We did not even play *Jacques a dit*! As for suggestions (e.g. *allons en ville, prenons quelque chose à boire*), these were never distinguished from the other imperatives. Unwittingly, we were led to believe that the forms ending in '-ons' were the equivalent of commands. Socially, they do not often fulfil this function. We were not explicitly shown that it was a way of making an invitation or suggestion. We knew the forms and the grammatical labels, but had very limited understanding of the scope of their function in the language.

Formal and informal grammar teaching

To establish exactly what we mean by the teaching of grammar, we distinguish between formal and informal teaching of grammar. The move away from the traditional 'formal' grammar teaching that concentrated on giving learners the rules is welcome. But, the formal teaching of rules and the explaining of structures may still be useful and should not be discarded as a matter of doctrine. It may help many learners to plan quite explicitly their own learning of the language, particularly as the more motivated learn more and are encouraged to become independent learners.

Informal grammar teaching provides learners with the chance to learn and use the language in authentic situations, the aim being that they learn to communicate competently. Structural forms are given to pupils so that they can perform language functions in communicative settings.

We believe that grammar teaching of both kinds has a place in the foreign language classroom. Of course, the trick is to get the balance right, so that one's approach takes account of individual learning preferences and the need for variety without the overuse of one favourite approach.

Which learners benefit from grammar?

At some time, a significant number of learners may benefit from focusing on the rules or patterns of language, but children with learning difficulties do not consciously apply abstract rules to produce utterances in a foreign language and may not benefit from the formal presentation of grammar. However, able pupils can benefit and may welcome formal explanations of grammatical rules and they may believe that they can apply knowledge of rules to productive use of language. A return to grammar-grind methods would not be productive, but a creative integration of grammar learning into the curriculum could be useful to some. For above-average learners this may involve the gradual acquisition of a metalanguage involving the principal parts of speech and the names of tenses 'one of the most central learning problems' (Dirven 1990).

Given that we are unable to identify the best way of teaching grammar for all learners, we might usefully engage our classes in a dialogue about ways in which they prefer to approach the learning task. It is our experience that teachers feel the need for grammar teaching. Foreign language course books offer grammar practice activities of the informal type as well as quite detailed formal descriptions of the language. Many publications address the grammar component of 11–14, GCSE and A Level courses, for example: Longman publications offer *The French Grammar File 11–14* (Berwick 1999); Marriott and Ribière (1998) offer GCSE and A Level French grammar books published by Longman and there are GCSE-related grammar guides for German (Price and Semple 1998) and Spanish (O'Connor 1998). To bridge the gap to A Level study, resources have been developed, for example, *Atelier Grammaire* (Hope and Hunt 1993). A lot of useful material has been developed in recent years.

Presentation of grammar

First of all, learners are introduced to a form (or forms), its meaning and its use in the language. The focus on form is not an end in itself but a necessary preparation for meaningful use in authentic contexts. There are many ways to present new language including:

- a written text with a particular grammar point to be underlined;
- a listening text exemplifying the function of a structure;
- a story that includes repetition of a particular structure;
- a visual (picture, flashcards, etc.) that illustrates the meaning of the structure;
- some real objects;
- a dialogue;
- a single sentence pattern on a board or OHP;
- the teacher using pupil activities and experiences to demonstrate the use of the language, e.g. the use of reflexives in the language of daily routine;
- a situational demonstration;
- children's explanations to each other;
- a formal explanation of a pattern or rule.

The more pupils are involved in exploration and discovery the more likely it is that they will grasp the shape of the language. Simply explaining the rule (in English or target language) and telling them to learn it is not usually very effective. Children are usually very willing and effective in helping one another learn. Their explanations are often clearer than those given by the teacher. Such a useful resource could be exploited to facilitate the understanding and learning of grammar.

Features of effective presentation

The presentation should be attention-grabbing. A stimulus, movement, noise, mime, contrast or something unexpected may help to grab and retain attention for long enough for the language point to be more easily memorised or recalled at a later date. The formal explanation of rules usually suffers a lack of quality in this respect.

The presentation should be uncluttered, with the meaning and use clear to learners (Harmer 1987). Instances of cluttering occur in some textbooks and where authentic texts are used for presentation. Care should be taken that the point you wish to focus on is readily accessible.

The presentation should be authentic in the sense that it provides a realistic context to show the meaning and use of the grammar point. This does not mean that children have to be forced to deduce the use from authentic written texts, radio broadcasts or websites. The presentation should allow the learner to see the potential communicative purpose of learning the new item, its function. This can be done from textbooks or from teacher-made material, from the board and from authentic sources.

Presentation quickly moves into the practice stage when the focus is on achieving accuracy in the grammar such that it can be difficult to decide what is presentation and what is practice. Once the meaning is clear and pupils become involved, then practice is taking place. In practical terms, the distinction between stages is of no real consequence.

Strategies for presentation

This section offers some practical examples of approaches to presenting grammar.

Symbols, charts and pictures

A teacher who wishes to present 'likes and dislikes' involving the use of the infinitive (for example, j'aime danser) might revise:

j'aime
j'adore   } with the symbols in Figure 7.1
je n'aime pas
je déteste

Figure 7.1

Then she might combine these with pictures of activities that interest young people. Once the structure has been practised, learners can be given a group card activity that allows them to practise the language independently of the teacher. In addition, pupils can be asked questions about themselves so that they have the chance to personalise their use of the language.

The symbols used can be very simple as in the following example, adapted from McKay (1985), in Figures 7.2 and 7.3. Gaps can be left in the presentation to allow pupils the chance to contribute and provide the missing elements.

+	−
mangez	ne mangez pas
entrez	n'entrez pas
quittez	....
écoutez	....
....	ne parlez pas

Figure 7.2

Instructions:
or, statements to questions through a board presentation or wallchart:

+	?
Il fait ses devoirs.	Est-ce qu'il fait ses devoirs?
Il aide ses parents.	Est-ce qu'il aide ses parents?
Elle respecte les professeurs.	Est-ce qu'elle respecte les professeurs?
Elle écoute en classe.	Est-ce qu' ....?
Elle	Est-ce qu'elle aime le jazz?

Figure 7.3

While Figure 7.4 below would not be an initial presentation of prepositional phrases, many pupils benefit from an explanation that summarises an otherwise complicated sequence, for example a display chart or overhead projection showing a rule/pattern with colour-coded sections (or different fonts, as in Figure 7.4) recording what has been taught during the course of a unit.

en face du	cinéma	**en face de la**	**gare**
	musée		**poste**
	stade		**mairie**
	supermarché		**banque**

en face de	**l'hôpital (m)**	en face des	magasins (m)
	l'hôtel de ville (m)		toilettes (f)
	l'épicerie (f)		téléphones (m)

Figure 7.4

Complementary visuals

These are particularly useful for the difficult area of link words like *pendant que* with imperfect and perfect tenses e.g.

Pendant que Paul marchait dans la forêt, il a vu un serpent

 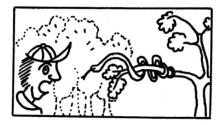

Figure 7.5

At higher levels, *malgré* can be introduced by way of a gradual progression from:

Il pleuvait hier soir. J'ai nagé dans le lac.
Qu'est-ce que tu as fait hier soir?
Malgré la pluie, j'ai nagé dans le lac.

Complementary visuals showing the following situations and activities provide appropriate contrasts for the use of *malgré*.

bad weather	/a plane taking off
a road accident	/someone continuing their journey
a headache	/someone studying
thick snow	/a child playing in the garden

You do not need to be an artist to mount such presentations. It is often possible to make useful combinations from existing sets of flashcards, wall pictures, course materials, or from sources such as Wright (1984), *A Thousand Pictures for Teachers to Copy*, Slater *et al*. (1987) *Borders, Layouts and Designs 1*, or Bastian and Best (1987) *Borders, Layouts and Designs 2*. Alternatively, many coursebooks exploit complementary visuals in this way, as do texts devoted to grammar teaching, for example, *Grammaire en Clair*, (Rogers and Long 1983), *Grammaire Directe* (Rogers 1999a) *Alles Klar* (Rogers and Long 1985) and *Grammatik Direkt* (Rogers 1999b). Such commercially produced materials, if affordable, can save hours of fruitless head-scratching for ideas to present and practise grammar. Alternatively, non-copyright material may be photocopied (reduced or blown up) directly onto acetate.

Overhead projector visuals

Visuals, drawn by the gifted or photocopied by the clumsy (from non-copyright sources) for use with the overhead projector can be used for a variety of presentations:

Transparency A   Transparency B

Figure 7.6

The pictures on Transparency A can be a vehicle for the presentation of verb forms in response to questions:

'Qu'est-ce qu'on fait comme distraction au collège?
Quel genre de club avez-vous dans votre collège?
Qu'est-ce qu'ils ont fait aujourd'hui?

Pupils can be presented with perfect tense forms beginning 'a' then 'ont', for example: *Marie a nagé. Robert a chanté. Mais, Anne et Claire ont joué au basket.*
Of course, the activity quickly becomes practice.

At more advanced levels, an ambitious presentation would be to overlay the pictures in A with Transparency B of the angry teacher whose tyres have been let down and teach or elicit what the people were doing at the time of the incident:

A deux heures, quelqu'un a dégonflé les pneus du directeur.

Que faisaient les enfants à deux heures?

Marie ne l'a pas fait. Elle travaillait dans un laboratoire. Elle faisait une expérience chimique etc.

It is not our intention to go through the whole repertoire of strategies for facilitating presentation when many of them are illustrated elsewhere in this book. They include gesture, demonstration, questioning and answering, puppet presentations. However, we do not wish to exclude from consideration formal approaches where they serve learners' needs, for instance, explanation of the 'system', noting a rule with examples, displays of language patterns on wallcharts (for example, tenses), working on grammar-related reading texts.

Grammar practice activities

The last two strategies mentioned above can be particularly useful at the practice stage. The wallchart, for example of verbs with *je suis* in the *passé composé* can serve as an effective visual aid when the focus is on that area of language.

A reading text (perhaps a story) allows for intensive study of particular features. A simple but effective activity is to ask pupils to underline or list certain features, for example,

- underline what the people did in this story (past historic/narrative past);
- underline the promises made in this song (future);
- list the things one can do in this village (modal);
- list the things they did not do on the holiday (negative narrative);
- underline the reasons (because + clause).

The text may well be teacher-made for the purpose of mediating the grammar in an accessible form, for example:

Bonjour Annie,

Bonne année à toi ! Merci pour ta jolie carte de Noël. J'espère que tu vas bien. J'ai passé les vacances de Noël de manière traditionnelle et j'en ai marre. Je trouve que c'est dégoûtant. C'est toujours la même chose ici.

Aujourd'hui, c'est le jour de l'an. Hier soir mon père a fumé des cigares et il a trop bu. Naturellement, il est malade ce matin. Je crois qu'il a vomi très fois. C'est dégoûtant. Ma mère est en colère et l'atmosphère est lamentable.

Par conséquent, j'ai pris des résolutions pour le Nouvel an.

1. Je vais partager tout avec mes frères.
2. Je ne vais plus me disputer avec eux.
3. Je ne vais jamais toucher à l'alcool.
4. Je ne vais jamais fumer.
5. Je ne vais pas embêter ma mère. (Mon père fait ça)
6. Je vais essayer de comprendre mon père.

C'est déjà assez, je pense. Comment est la vie en Angleterre? Comme tu le sais, ma famille est bizarre.

Écris-moi vite,

Au revoir,

Étienne

Figure 7.7

A range of activities can follow through which pupils can:

- identify four things that Etienne has resolved not to do;
- say what he is going to do.

After this, pupils can be asked to express some of their own positive intentions (if they have any) and

- say what they are determined not to do in the future;
- compose a reply to the letter which includes a brief account of how things are going and what resolutions they have made.

Another possibility is to ask pupils to study the features of a text and attempt to discover the general pattern or rule. The text must give various examples of the rule, for instance of German agreement or of a tense such as the future in French. This can be a pair or group activity, allowing learners to speculate on the organisation of the language. For this same purpose, presentation of single sentence patterns on the board may be very effective. Subsequent imitation of patterns can help many learners to retain them particularly for purposes of writing:

Qu'est-ce que tu as fait le weekend dernier?
J'ai visité un château.

acheté/un ordinateur   *joué/dans le parc*
regardé/un film   *fait/des courses en ville*

Most of the activities mentioned so far in this section concentrate on the practice of forms. It is essential that pupils be given the chance to engage in meaningful activities that involve an information gap, some element of personalisation or some exchange of opinions and ideas. These activities are similar to tasks exemplified in Chapters 3 and 4. Many of the examples are standard classroom fare, well-used in 'traditional' foreign language teaching, but it is still worth reminding ourselves of some of them.

The questionnaire

Questionnaires can be used to practise language from all areas of experience: likes/dislikes, preferences, personal information, daily routine, to find out what people can and cannot do:

Name	schwimmen	tanzen	skilaufen	judo spielen	gitarre spielen

Figure 7.8

Find out what your partner has written

This interactive game is very useful (and enjoyable) for the practice of questions, suggestions, for example:

Pupils are given the sentences in the respective target language and asked to write their own endings, without showing their partner:

Ieri, sono andato (a). . .   *Gestern bin ich . . . gegangen*
Lì, ho comprato . . .   *Ich habe dort . . . gekauft.*
Poi, ho incontrato . . .   *Dann habe ich . . . begegnet.*
Più tardi, ho deciso di . . .   *Ich bin mich entschieden . . .*

Secretly, they write their own endings or inserts to each phrase. Then, their partner has to guess what has been written using the forms:

Ieri, sei andato(a) . . . or   *Gestern bist du . . . gefahren.*

This generates a lot of speculation and can be fun to engage in.

Information gap

For the practice of third-person question forms and description, simple grids can be used:

	1	2	3	4
Nome	Carla Rossi		Paul Soler	
Età				29
Città	Monaco		Toronto	
Nazionalità		australiana	canadese	tunisino
Professione	farmacista	insegnante		

	1	2	3	4
Nome		Mary Banks		Ben Masood
Età	28	34	32	
Città		Melbourne		Lione, Francia
Nazionalità	italiana			
Professione			m eccanico	falegname

Figure 7.9

This allows for controlled practice of question forms:

Come si chiama?　　　　　*Quanti anni ha?*
Dove abita?　　　　　　　*Che fa nella vita?*
E, la sua nazionalità?

and the appropriate answers to them.

Controlled practice in pairs

To complement the summary chart that exemplifies the use of *en face*, a controlled pair activity might preface an authentic use of maps:
　　Pupil A has the task :

A. *Demande à ton partenaire où se trouve*　　*la pharmacie.*
　　　　　　　　　　　　　　　　　　　　　le commissariat.
　　　　　　　　　　　　　　　　　　　　　la banque.
　　　　　　　　　　　　　　　　　　　　　la poste.

Pupil B is given an instruction and a simple map (or asked to make one with the target vocabulary):

B. *Répond à ton partenaire. Donne-lui les informations nécessaires.*

la banque	le tabac	le café	l'épicerie	la pharmacie

le garage	la poste	l'hotel	le commissariat	les toilettes

These tasks perhaps do not relate readily to the area traditionally associated with 'grammar' teaching. Nevertheless, they are opportunities to practise in a meaningful way what has been taught. They may well have been preceded by a grammatical explanation (even one with labels like 'verb'!). They are useful because the practice can be devolved to pupils. This may cause unease because checks for accuracy are limited when pupils are engaged in pair/group speaking tasks. A traditional solution to this problem is to ask pupils to write some examples of what they have spoken, for example:

Ecrivez cinq phrases avec 'en face' pour décrire la rue.

Too much of this type of practice would certainly demotivate, but many pupils will welcome the opportunity to have some correct phrases written down, to act as models of accurate sentences.

Teaching and learning styles

Perhaps the key to successful grammar teaching is to assure a balance of teacher-led and pupil-centred activities. In this way, the teacher has the opportunity to do some monitoring of the level of accuracy, providing corrective models where appropriate. Very often, there is no substitute for a lively, well-directed question and answer session led by the teacher.

When classes take this form, it is important to make sure that all pupils get the chance to say something. They should all realise that they will be given the chance. Ideally, no one should feel left out and all members of the class should be able to offer responses at different levels of ability. A balance of carefully-directed yes/no, either/or, true/false and open-ended questions may help. When evaluating such phases of lessons, it is important to review the spread of interaction around the classroom, considering who benefits most from such teacher-led activity. Everyone should experience some success in using the language.

Towards the end of the lesson, the teacher can ask for those who have not said anything to volunteer for a turn. This ensures that everyone has a chance and shows that you do not just wish to include the livelier members of the group. When asking for responses it is important to show genuine interest in the reply, particularly where the answer tells you something personal to the learner, for example, in response to:

Quelle est ta musique préférée?
Que penses-tu du jazz?
Qu'est-ce que tu as fait pendant les vacances?

An alternative to straight questions is the use of requests:

Est-ce que tu peux me décrire ta maison?
Est-ce que tu voudrais parler de tes passetemps?

or, polite instructions:

Dis-moi ce que tu penses de la musique classique, s'il te plait? Parle-moi un peu de ton village.

Drills can occasionally be useful in the practice of grammar. They can be prompted by pictures, gestures, actions and verbal cues, for example:

Model: *Est-ce que tu voudrais aller au théâtre avec moi, ce soir?*
      (Pupils repeat this sentence)

The teacher can then call out prompts which pupils substitute in the appropriate space in the sentence. They can do this chorally or individually, or a mixture of both:

au cinéma	*à la plage*	(Pupils substitute the phrases)
au café	*à la patinoire*	
au concert	*à la disco*	
au match de tennis		

or the teacher might focus on a different part of the structure:

ce weekend?
demain?
cet après-midi?
demain soir?
samedi soir?

which pupils substitute.

Alternatively, the teacher could hold up a series of flashcards showing a cinema, café, beach, disco, concert, tennis match. This might be appropriate practice for the group, if they had recently been taught the grammar of *au/à la,* etc. though it leaves more scope for error in pupil replies. They could then go to work on dialogues or messages where this particular structure and function are involved. To conclude, they may be given guidance in writing the target structures, for example, on notes inviting people out.

The drills should not go on too long (usually six to eight prompts) as they quickly become repetitive and monotonous. Where possible, they should move from repetition or straight substitution to more meaningful responses. A sequence might move through the following stages (adapted from Dakin 1973, p. 67):

Target phrases (on the board):

Voici un bon livre.	*Bien, je voudrais le lire.*
Voici un bon disque.	*Bien, je voudrais l'écouter.*
Voici une belle chemise.	*Bien, je voudrais l'essayer.*
La peinture est belle.	*Bien, je voudrais la voir.*

Pupils listen to each prompt and repeat in chorus. Then, the teacher calls out further prompts and pupils volunteer to respond:

Il y a un bon film à la télé. _____

Ce disque de Madonna est génial. _____

Le magazine est intéressant. _____

Ma maison est grande. _____

Voici Anne. Elle est très intelligente. _____

Voici une belle jupe. _____

To follow, the teacher might hold up a series of objects and elicit similar pattern practice, using visual rather than verbal cues. After this, pupils should move on to using the language in more meaningful circumstances, perhaps responding to adverts for films, books, records, clothes, toys and games by expressing opinions and wishes.

Situations can offer useful illustrative contexts for drills in oral or written form. They can be quite simple, focusing on use of adjectives, for example:

Jacques fait beaucoup de sport.	*Il est très sportif.*
Anne fait beaucoup de sport.	*Elle* _____
Hélène n'a pas dormi.	*Elle* _____

Robert n'a pas dormi. _____

Robert ne travaille pas. _____

Anne gagne beaucoup d'argent. _____

Or, they can be more detailed:

Exemple: Monsieur Bertrand habite un petit appartement. Il rêve d'une grande maison à la campagne. Il regarde les photos dans les agences immobilières, mais les maisons coûtent très cher.

S'il était riche, il aurait une grande maison à la campagne.

Pamela a un vieux clou, une Renault 5 qui a quinze ans. Elle regarde les nouvelles voitures dans les garages. Pour elle, ce n'est pas possible parce qu'elle est étudiante à l'université.

Si elle ....

Claire déteste vivre en France. Elle en a marre du matérialisme occidental. Elle rêve de l'Egypte. Malheureusement, elle ne peut pas quitter ses parents.

Si elle ....

For teacher-led activities, the OHP is a very versatile device that can target verb forms. In the following example the teacher has the option of pointing to a person and an activity, eliciting appropriate responses in the tense being practised or calling out a number and the name(s) of the person around the picture. Pupils then produce the correct pronoun (*il/elle/ils/elles*) and verb in response:

Figure 7.10

Using the numbers gives the teacher mobility, allowing her the chance to stray away from the whirring overhead projector.

Those who, like us, cannot draw or do not have access to an OHP or photocopier may be able to divide the whiteboard in order to orchestrate practice. Here are some examples of the possibilities:

	Voici Christine. Elle travaille dans une agence de voyage.	Voici Roland. Il est mécanicien.
Devoirs	- vendre des billets - travailler avec un ordinateur - servir aux clients	- réparer des autos - changer les pneus - nettoyer le garage - répondre au téléphone
Désirs	- sortir avec Christopher - aller à la plage - gagner beaucoup d'argent	- jouer au tennis - sortir avec Christine - écrire des poésies

Figure 7.11 (adapted from Harmer 1987, p. 42)

Such prompts can be used for teacher led question and answer work focusing on:

Qu'est-ce que Christine doit faire?
Qu'est-ce que Roland doit faire?
Qu'est-ce qu'elle/il voudrait faire?
Qu'est-ce qu'il/elle veut faire?

or

Qu'est-ce qu'il/elle ne peut pas faire?

Noughts and crosses (recommended in Harmer 1987, p. 48) is also a useful teacher-led game that can focus on almost any aspect of grammar, especially at higher levels, for example:

1 veut	2. voulons	3. veulent
4. veux	5. voulez	6. veux
7. veux	8. veulent	9. voulez

Figure 7.12

Pupils in teams choose a number and make an utterance (positive, negative, or question form according to the rules agreed), using the form in their box. This can help to focus on person and form without being too monotonous. In the same vein, prepositions, pronouns, past participles and question words (such as *pourquoi, comment, où, quand, qui, que*) could be set for whatever level required.

Helping pupils learn grammar

Note-taking

At times, pupils desire an explanation of how the language works which they can understand. It may be necessary to teach the quickest and most effective way of making notes for foreign language grammar and monitor the way students are making their notes. Many children rely on note-taking to assist learning and we feel that many learners benefit from gradually acquiring a battery of grammatical labels. The notes need not take particularly long-winded form. Teachers must decide which is more appropriate: pupils making their own notes or simply copying those of their teacher. Where appropriate, pupils can record the pattern through isolated models which are highlighted in some way, for example:

Present conditionals

S'il pleut, je **resterai** à la maison.
Si le soleil brille, **j'irai** à la plage.
or for Type 2 conditionals (*Si j'étais riche . . .*) through the noting of some situations as outlined above.

   A useful strategy recommended by Ellis and Sinclair (1989, p. 47) sees English grammar classified under the headings:

| Facts | Patterns | Choices |

Facts correspond to exceptions or to things that simply have to be learnt; *patterns* refer to the predictable regular forms of morphology and syntax; and, language users make *choices* (for example, between tenses, depending on their purpose and meaning). Occasionally, this may have potential for pupils' note-taking in the foreign language classroom, for example:

Future tense

Facts	Pattern	Choices
J'aurai	All other 'er/ir'	Two ways:
J'irai	infinitives +	
Je serai	*ai*	*Je vais* + infinitive
Je ferai	*as*	e.g. *Je vais sortir*
J'enverrai	*a*	or
Je verrai	*ons*	*Je sortirai*
Je viendrai	*ez*	
Je tiendrai	*ont*	
Je mourrai		

Facts	Pattern	Choices
Je courrai	e.g. *je parlerai*	
Je saurai	*je finirai*	
Je pourrai		
Je voudrai		
Je devrai	'Re' verbs such as	
	vendre lose the 'e'.	
	e.g. *je vendrais*	

The facts have to be learnt, the patterns can be imitated and exploited, while the appropriate choices have to be made. This does not solve all learner difficulties, but some may benefit from such an alternative form of notes. The format may help learners to cope with irregularity in some aspects of the language, for example, past participles.

Organisation of notes

If pupils do keep a record of models with labels, they would almost certainly benefit from indexing their notes in their folder or exercise book. Having a record of what they have noted with page numbers will develop organisational and reference skills. As a result, the use of textbooks for grammatical reference will become more effective. Modern coursebooks have grammar sections or supplementary resources devoted to grammar but pupils need guidance on ways in which such reference material can help them. If a writing task is set which involves the use of the reflexive form, (for example an account of a daily routine), preparation for this may take the form of finding the relevant section in the textbook. Guidance with textbook use will support and promote independent use of reference material.

Classification

Classification tasks can help to clarify patterns and usage. For instance, studying a text, pupils are required to list noun phrases in which adjectives are used:

Feminine		Masculine	
Singular	Plural	Singular	Plural

or, they read a text to list the adverbs used in it, then list the adjectives from which they derive. They could then possibly explore issues related to word order, often difficult and neglected.

The possibilities are numerous: studying a recipe to list the instructions and objects, reading a letter to list facts and reasons. The study of a brief story can have pupils categorising past time forms as continuous or completed activities in the past. The key point is that pupils should be engaged in the exploration and discovery of the language, not listening to abstract rules.

Visual support in the classroom

Wallcharts can support both oral and written work provided that they are prominently displayed and relatively uncluttered. The use of symbols may help learning:

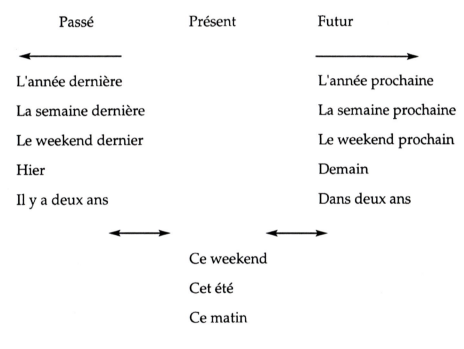

Figure 7.13

Such a device can support pupils' writing responses to the standard letters that ask them to answer queries from sympathetic pen-friends, here promoting and supporting the use of time adverbials.

Key forms such as the verbs taking *être* in the past tense can be displayed for the duration of a unit of work which has as its focus the use of these forms, for example, a unit which investigates holiday experiences. In addition, the learning of past participles can be facilitated in this manner.

Model texts on the walls can also be helpful, for example, pictures of activities with appropriate captions, or pictures of people accompanied by physical descriptions. Classroom rules displayed in the target language demonstrate the use of forms such as *il faut, on ne doit pas, verboten, non si può, si può, è vietato.* Opportunities to provide such visual support are worth the necessary investment in time. Very often, pupils are keen to make posters for the classroom. Why not steer them grammatically?

Pupils explaining grammar

With abler pupils, there is much to be gained from encouraging them to give oral explanations to their classroom peers. This has at least two benefits:

1. the teacher can gauge the extent to which the grammatical input has been understood and
2. the pupils hear (and probably give more attention to) a peer explanation of a grammatical point.

In a sense, one might describe such a task as being both a learning and communicative activity, involving pupils in verbalising their understanding and explaining this to peers.

Conclusion

Grammar has been retrieved from its marginalised position in the naughty corner. It is taught and must be taught. Even when unfashionable, a vast number of teachers taught grammar, sometimes guiltily apologising or even pretending that they were not 'doing grammar'. It has an important place. Perhaps it should not be the starting point or the sole focus as in times past, but the study of how to help our pupils to approach the learning and use of grammar is healthy. In this chapter we have considered some of the approaches that we have found useful.

Chapter 8
Vocabulary

The time allocated to the first language in the secondary curriculum leaves pupils with an immense vocabulary learning task, at least 2,000 words to attain higher level GCSE standard, far more for 16–19 programmes. The basic 11–16 memory load is over five words per hour, without consideration of use and inflection. The second language, often German or Spanish, has to compete but in even less time, sometimes as little as half.

Little wonder that learners have occasionally found themselves issued with GCSE vocabulary lists to work on privately. These are the successors of the old vocabulary textbooks used in the days of O Level and CSE, when bewildered pupils fell victim to unknown words and phrases, for example *hisser la voile* in a French CSE examination paper! The National Curriculum does not specify vocabulary content, but the Programme of Study limits what is to be covered. GCSE vocabulary lists (for example those provided by the NEAB) provide essential and useful guidance for the planning of vocabulary teaching and learning.

The burden of learning vocabulary is inevitable. You cannot use the language effectively without words. Perhaps as a result of the daunting size of the task, the learning of vocabulary has been a little neglected, but there are excellent sources of advice on the teaching of vocabulary (Gairns and Redman 1986, Allen 1983, for example).

Selection of vocabulary to help pupils learn

It is clear that some words and phrases are potentially more important than others, for example, high frequency items like the function words:

> *et, donc, qui, que, si*   or   *und, aber, wer, wann, weil.*

Content words should be chosen on the basis of their potential use by the pupils. Items that are used in many contexts (home, school, public buildings) must be given high priority so:

une table, une chaise, un mur, une porte, une fenêtre, une chambre, would normally take priority over

une table de chevet, un porte-chapeaux, une ottomane.

This may seem obvious but we recall the forced learning of the French for cock-chafer, cicada and other creatures, leaving school at 18 not only not knowing what such creatures looked like but also ignorant of the French for household items like frying pan, bottle opener, tin opener and corkscrew.

What is to be learnt?

When meeting a new word pupils have to learn what the item means and how it is used (Harmer 1991), either being or becoming aware of possible inflections and the sentence grammar governing the item. Inevitably, when selecting words or phrases, teachers decide which high frequency items require this full treatment. Such items need to be taught in context, with learners given adequate opportunities to use the words in appropriate settings and communicative activities.

Organisation of vocabulary books

The identification of high frequency function words, high frequency content words and low frequency items may help to divide up the learning for pupils. If they use the traditional vocabulary books, they could be asked to divide it into sections:

1. Pages for key function words that often escape, e.g. narrative link words: *mais, d'abord, puis, donc.*
2. A section for each of the anticipated content areas to be covered, for example, school life, home life, media, the international world, etc.
3. A section for low frequency items.
4. A section for miscellaneous words and phrases.
5. An idiom bank.
6. An optional section of grammatical functions, especially verbs, adjectives and prepositions.

Such a division may be an improvement on the haphazard and often disordered noting of words that we recall from school days, for example:

la familia	the family
un espantapajaros	a scarecrow
un gitano	a gypsy
un hermano	brother
una hermana	sister
el cuerpo	the body
un diccionario	a dictionary
una muchacha	a girl
comer	to eat

While such haphazard organisation may be necessary sometimes, it is believed that learning is made easier when words are grouped under a topic or theme.

Presenting and recording language in ways which might assist recall can be explored, for example, the following organisation of words that can be grouped under 'family' or presented in a family tree would probably be more learnable:

la familia, el padre, la madre, un hijo, una hija, un(a) hermano(a)

Or, words can be grouped in some sort of 'natural' order as with parts of the face or body:

La tête et le visage	**Le corps**
les cheveux	le cou
le front	une épaule une épaule
une oreille les yeux une oreille	le bras le bras
le nez	la poitrine
une joue une joue	la main droite la main gauche
la bouche	l'estomac
le menton	une jambe une jambe
le cou	un pied un pied

adapted from Holden (1999).

Helping pupils learn

Teachers have always offered advice for strategies on learning vocabulary: ten minutes a day before going to bed; friends testing one another; putting new words on a notice board at home; standing v-shaped cards up on the window-sill. All such strategies may help pupils.

Teachers can also help their pupils in the classroom by seeking the most useful ways to record and revise vocabulary (word webs, games, brainstorms). Many of our pupils will only learn in the classroom (not all have the will or inclination to study words privately), so a variety of strategies is needed to maintain interest and encourage positive learning habits.

The value of regular revision and recycling cannot be overstated, particularly with the most-needed words. Naturally, progress will be easier with those who are motivated by personal satisfaction or persuaded of the joys of word learning!

For important words, it is advisable that an example of use be included in the vocabulary book. Learners need opportunities to learn vocabulary in context, use new words and reactivate them at early opportunities especially when they are key content or function words. For concrete vocabulary, activities which involve touching the objects may aid teaching and learning (Allen 1983, p. 24) for some learners.

Other learners might suggest that conscious learning out of context is also helpful so we would not condemn private word learning followed by checks or brief tests. Such procedures help to reactivate the words and phrases. Knowledge can be checked by brainstorming from a topic web, as in the following example:

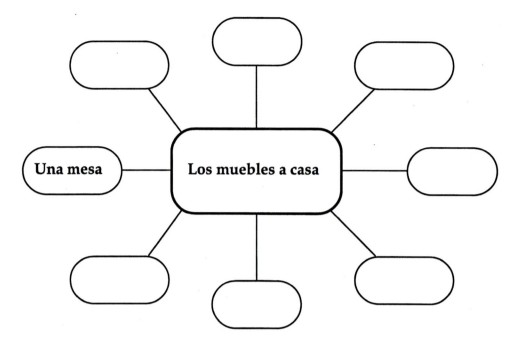

Figure 8.1

Pupils are asked to recall and write in the topic words that they have focused on. This recall activity is useful for practice as well and can be done in pairs or small groups. Other pencil and paper tests, for example using picture prompts, prompts in English, gap-filling tasks and multiple-choice techniques can be used as checks for vocabulary learning. To succeed, pupils must be guided in their learning, that is to say, given attainable targets, not the learning of several pages from notebooks.

Visual support in the classroom can be of great benefit, for example to assist pupils with their writing of a report about an accident. The following chart can be produced very quickly on the board or OHP:

Lieu	Séquence	Résultat
là-bas	d'abord	donc
dans la rue	puis	par conséquent
partout	ensuite	par suite de l'accident
dans cet endroit	plus tard	malheureusement; à cause de
à l'hôpital	cependant	malgré

Figure 8.2

Key transactional vocabulary can be supported by cut-out visual aids (on sugar paper) in the classroom, for example a drawing of a tent with the key campsite vocabulary or a large bottle with possible drinks:

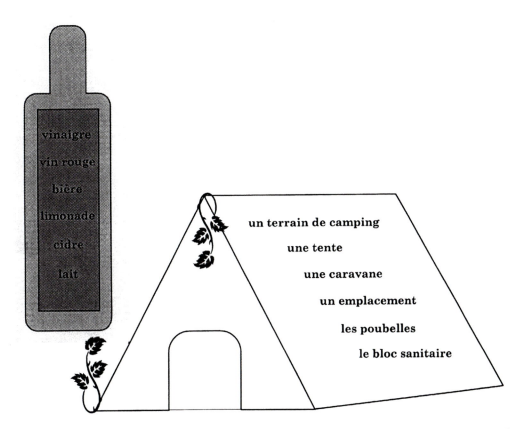

vinaigre

vin rouge

bière

limonade

cidre

lait

un terrain de camping

une tente

une caravane

un emplacement

les poubelles

le bloc sanitaire

Figure 8.3

There are many obvious examples of this approach:

- crockery and cutlery words suspended on a plate from the ceiling;
- a blown-up menu to remind pupils of food items;
- signs can be placed around the modern languages classrooms;
- the drawing of a house with the rooms labelled;
- a train engine and carriage carrying the key words for buying tickets;
- a labelled picture of a skeleton;
- a chart of facial expressions using drawings and appropriate adjectives (*triste, heureux, souriant*, etc.).

To ease the burden, less 'willing' learners may occasionally be given the option of learning any 10 out of 30 possible items. Hopefully, this choice will lead them to learn something of value.

Presentation of new vocabulary

Concrete nouns

Much new vocabulary is presented with structures that have been, or are being, taught. This allows pupils the opportunity to engage in practice activities that require the use of the new items. In the early stages of learning the language, pupils are usually presented with a lot of concrete nouns, for example:

> *Je voudrais* + items of food
> *Elle porte* + items of clothing
> *J'ai/Nous avons* + personal possessions

In these circumstances, presentation is usually supported by the use of:

- pictures,
- magazine cut-outs,
- OHP drawings,
- flashcards,
- gestures,
- realia, and sometimes
- translation.

Occasionally, this may lead to an unusual amount of drawing in the language classroom, as pupils note the new vocabulary. The more elaborate and time-consuming drawings are perhaps better set for homework. Furthermore, when cognates are presented, for example, *ein Kaffee, ein Coca, ein Telefon, ein Haus*, drawings are perhaps an unnecessary indulgence.

There can also be quite a lot of copying from the board or OHP. Copying is a useful activity offering pupils the opportunity to record an item correctly but copying from an often hurriedly written board can be very difficult. It is important that pupils are not presented with too many new items to note and that these be clearly printed in lower case (unless, as with German nouns, place names, exclamations, upper case is appropriate) and presented on a clear background. Otherwise, errors are inevitably widespread. To save pupils the stress of copying from the board, pre-prepared worksheets are a safer bet for the promotion of accurate copying. Figure 8.4 would complement a flashcard presentation of crockery and cutlery vocabulary.

This copying activity is a little more challenging because the learners have to match the word to the picture but the words are not a long distance away on a board. Even so, it is likely that there will be errors. If pupils agree, peer checking in pairs can help to correct this immediately.

Despite the apparent simplicity of the task, for some learners, this level of writing can be daunting. Pupils with difficulties in writing may need to have the captions already written so that they can match the caption to the picture.

It is worth remembering that average learners cannot cope with a learning load of more than six to eight new items per lesson, whether an item is a single word, a phrase or short sentence. However, the burden may be eased with the judicious presentation of cognates which help to support learning so long as pupils are given the chance to develop awareness of cognate relationships (see Chapter 5).

un plato	*un cuchillo*	*un tenedor*	*un mantel*	*una taza*
un vaso	*una cuchara*	*un bol*	*un platillo*	

Figure 8.4

Verbs

In the early stages the meaning of many verbs (with persons or pronouns being taught) can be presented through pictures, flashcards, mime, gestures, demonstrations, acting as well as translation. Consider the various possibilities in relation to the following groups:

sie/er schwimmt, tanzt, singt, sieht fern.

er/sie lacht, lachelt, weint, schreit.

*il **quitte** la salle, il **laisse** le paquet sur la table, il **sort** du   collège.*

Many meanings will become clear from the situation in which the verbs are taught, though this will not show the verb's full potential as in:

*Le train **part** à quelle heure?*

The verb in bold, for many pupils, takes on the role of 'departs' in English. It is important that the word be presented in other situations, not just in contrast to 'arrive' at the railway station.

The presentation of verbs begins to get a little tougher when we move towards the less concrete activities or abstract concepts such as thinking, remembering, recalling, believing, hoping, trying, yearning, dreaming, suggesting and many more.

These can be presented through demonstration, explanation, definition, or situational contexts with pupils guessing; we may also use written texts with pupils inferring the meaning and at higher levels we may even use synonyms. Most commonly (and again it is inevitable given the pressures of time), the more abstract concepts may be presented most effectively through translation. This is effective so long as opportunities are built in for the verb's exemplification and use if it is to become part of the pupils' active target language vocabulary. At higher levels, students need to be made aware that the semantic range of apparently similar words varies across languages. The following phrases give an illustration of the challenges facing learners: *prix intéressants; conséquences fâcheuses; dégats importants.*

Adjectives

The presentation of adjectives will usually occur in context, perhaps in reading. As with nouns and verbs many will be cognates of English words and pupils should be encouraged to find patterns and make predictions, for example:

généreux, courageux, patient, impatient.

Many adjectives can be presented in contrastive pairs with their opposite:

gross/klein; sauber/schmutzig; voll/leer; kalt/heiss.

Again, the meaning can be seen through pictures, gesture, guessing from context and translation.

Languages provide stimulating opportunities for word-building activities, for example deriving nouns from adjectives:

bon – bonté	*beau – beauté*
honnête – honnêteté	*sale – saleté*

or, perhaps more commonly, adverbs from adjectives, in those languages where this occurs for example *natural/naturelle/naturellement; doux/douce/doncement.*

At Key Stage 4 and beyond, meeting new adjectives provides an opportunity for the presentation of nouns for noting along with the adjective. The resulting awareness of relationships can ease the burden of covering the vocabulary of the areas of experience of the National Curriculum, GCSE or A Level syllabus:

poli – la politesse	*doux, douce – la douceur*
cruel(le) – la cruauté	*violent – la violence*
triste – la tristesse	

Failure to develop word-building habits can limit pupils' capacity to cope when reading and listening in communicative contexts. Useful advice on communication strategies with vocabulary is given in GCSE examination syllabuses, for instance the descriptions of the Northern Examining Assessment Board (NEAB). In addition, a range of publications offer support for the development of wordpower, for example, Lanzer and Gordon (1995) in the Vocabulary Builder series of publications.

Practice

Basic level activities

Vocabulary-building practice can usefully concentrate on pupils' efforts to use the vocabulary to fulfil purposes, for example, with concrete items, guessing what is hidden in a bag, or what is on the flashcard which the teacher keeps hidden. Other ideas that work include:

Kim's Game

Objects are displayed on a table. The teacher practises the language by question/answer, true/false activities then hides the objects in a box or under a cloth. Pupils recall the items they have seen.

Chain Drill

Pupils in groups form a chain passing words to the next person and adding another in a given topic area, for example, with furniture:

Pupil A: *Ein Tisch*
Pupil B: *Ein Tisch, ein Stuhl . . .*
Pupil C: *Ein Tisch, ein Stuhl, ein Teppich . . .*

Lucky Dip

Groups of pupils brainstorm the words they know for a topic, for example, health and fitness. They write the words on slips of paper and place them in an envelope. They can refer to notebooks for guidance (an early encouragement of reference skills). The envelope is then exchanged with that of another group. Each member of the group has to extract slips in turn and use the word in a correct utterance, for example;

   dos: j'ai mal au dos.

A correct utterance means that the pupil keeps the paper. The group member who ends up with most paper is the winner. (Adapted from Allen 1983, pp. 50–51.)

A variation is a group composition activity based on a set number of items chosen from the envelope. This may involve the group in the preparation of a dialogue, message, letter or even a story to be swapped with that composed by another group. Of course, the contents of the envelope can be entirely teacher-directed, involving pictures or symbols instead of words, where appropriate.

At higher levels, students can be asked to review the vocabulary introduced in a topic. Then, in pairs or small groups they note on slips of paper some items from the topic. The vocabulary items are collected, put in a bag or box and students draw out words with which they have to make sentences. This can be a game for teams or groups. It can even be set as a writing activity.

When learners are used to this activity it can be made more complicated with groups revising more than one vocabulary area, then being asked to select words from two or three topics. It is a game that will work at any level from elementary to advanced.

Matching

Pupils match pictures to words, words to definitions or words to illustrative situations, for example:

Quest'uomo è senza soldi. E molto	povero.
Dieser Junge arbeitet nicht in der Klasse. Er ist	faul.

Figure 8.5

Sorting games

Pupils are given vocabulary items on cards or slips of paper and they are asked to categorise them in some way, under topics, under key words or pictures. This sorting can be done individually, in pairs, or in groups.

Nella cucina	*Nella camera*	*Nel salotto*
una toleta	*un letto*	*un armadio*
un acquaio	*un frigorifero*	*un forno*
una sedia	*un divano*	*uno scaffale*
una poltrona		

Or, pupils are given a blank menu, then asked to order cards or labels in order to make the day's menu, under starters, main courses, desserts, drinks and so on.

Ordering

Words can be ordered on a scale to show their relative value according to size, frequency, intensity, rapidity, for example, placing words in their order of frequency on the rungs of a ladder. Sometimes a rung may hold more than one word:

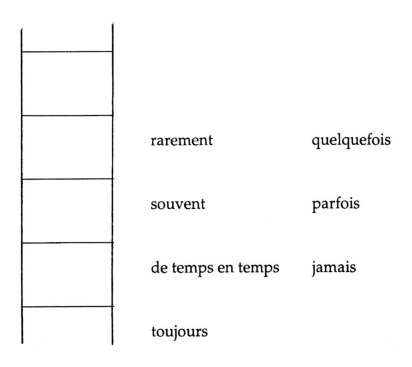

rarement   quelquefois

souvent   parfois

de temps en temps   jamais

toujours

Figure 8.6

This activity can operate at higher levels with learners sorting groups of related adjectives, for instance, *mauvais, méchant, épouvantable, affreux, abominable, terrible* for degree of evil.

Strategies for higher level

Many of the techniques already mentioned, for example, matching (newspaper headlines to articles, standard words or phrases to idioms, words to definitions), and ordering are appropriate if adapted to the correct level. At higher levels, the regular availability and use of dictionaries should enhance the quality and scope of the learning experience.

Cloze

Older learners are presented with a new text which has every tenth, or eighth or seventh word missing, depending on ability. They have to suggest possibilities for the gaps (which might be numerous). Again, the availability of dictionaries allows for the practice of reference skills to supply possibilities for the gaps. Variations are possible, for example: with the missing words available at the foot of the text, students choose from the given possibilities; or they use resources (their own knowledge, dictionaries, textbooks, exercise books, etc.) to plug the gaps.

Word roses

Choose a text and select 7 or 8 items of vocabulary and present them in a word rose, for example an article about an incident involving military aircraft:

un siège éjectable

le tour de contrôle   *heurta*
une crise cardiaque   *des témoins*
les services d'urgence   *pitoyable*
une enquête

Students are asked to predict the content of the text in speech or writing on the basis of the given words or phrases. If in doubt about any of the words they can use dictionaries to help. They are then given the text for comparison. An alternative is to have students use each item of vocabulary to report an incident they have seen in real life or on TV. Completed reports can be exchanged for comment or addition by peers.

Grids

A collocation grid offers the chance for students to speculate on possible lexical combinations in the foreign language. They can check for patterns of collocation when reading or using dictionaries, with useful or common collocations for use in their own writing.

	la bouche	la voix	la tête	la main	les yeux	les épaules	l'oreille	les sourcils
hausser								
secouer								
dresser								
froncer								
ouvrir								

Figure 8.7

A synonym grid may help learners to see the relationships between words. They match the words that have similar meanings in the grid:

	charmant	vain	intéressé	mesquin	orgueill-eux	craintif
timide						/
agréable	/					
égoïste		?	/			
avare				/		
fier					/	
superbe		/			/	

Figure 8.8

The use of grids can be effective in promoting the use of monolingual and bilingual dictionaries. Students group the items in synonym groups, then look for examples of usage in dictionaries so they can explore differences in nuance and use. They can explore how different words collocate.

Finding equivalents

Students are given a French text to read, for instance, about a shopping excursion. They are asked to locate and underline words/phrases which mean:

- *l'argent*
- *les provisions*
- *manquer d'argent*
- *des marchandises à prix réduits*
- *prendre quelque chose à manger.*

Categorisation

A number of variations are used, for example, arranging words into formal/neutral/informal, (Wallace 1982) good/bad or wise/unwise categories. Another way is to ask students to associate adjectives with roles, for instance:

Guarda le parole qui sotto. Mettile sotto le professioni secondo le esigenze del lavoro:

professore	postino	giornalista	soldato	direttrice di banca	medico	primo ministro

Si deve essere

paziente	crudele	ambizioso(a)	coraggioso(a)
buono(a)	simpatico(a)	ubbidiente	organizzato(a)
piccolo(a)	umile	generoso(a)	gentile
energico(a)	timido(a)	giovane	sensible
sincero(a)	disonesto	onesto(a)	ricco(a)
ostinato(a)	rapido(a)	spensierato(a)	forte
egoista	vecchio	fortunato (a)	triste

Figure 8.9

Students can be asked to comb texts to categorise new or known words in similar fashion. In groups, they have to justify their choices, thus forcing the practice of the target vocabulary.

Adjective game

Each student is given five slips or cards from a pack or 40 or 50 personal adjectives similar to those in the above categorisation activity. Students take turns to pick a slip or card. They can exchange three adjectives, but must then declare the hand and use the words to describe themselves. Their descriptions can be challenged by other members of the group. If a competitive edge is desired, a chairperson can award 'good' challengers opponents' cards, the winner being the one with the most cards after the justifications have finished.

Problem solving

A problem-solving activity using authentic resources (if available) could involve group or pair work:

Faites une liste des besoins d'une famille refugiée qui arrive en France. Puis, trouvez les adresses nécessaires dans les pages jaunes. (Adapted from Allen 1983, p. 69.)

If the yellow pages are not available, then an information brochure may be sufficient for the task or, if available, students can seek the information from the Internet. Simpler tasks can be set that involve gap-filling (appropriate addresses, necessary items, for examples, *permis de séjour, carte d'identité*), or ranking possible items for the family in order of importance or matching problems to solutions.

Examples of vocabulary activities abound in recent publications. The above are just offered as a reminder of some of the possibilities. We hope that they will encourage approaches more imaginative than the issuing of vocabulary lists, that learners will be given opportunities to process and use new language items in a wide range of contexts and in a variety of activities.

Section 4: Assessment and recording

Chapter 9

Assessment and recording achievement in foreign languages

Assessment and recording are areas of teaching which are laden with theory, jargon, controversy and misunderstanding. We should indeed be innovative if we could avoid all four of these, but we shall try to keep them to the minimum. Teachers who wish to find a more detailed theoretical guide to assessment and recording are advised to refer to more specialised works such as *Assessment in action* (Lee and Dickson 1989). Various publications by the DfEE set out current statutory requirements. These are often clear and are obligatory reading for most teachers as they help to dispel many of the misconceptions in this area of work.

The aim of this chapter is to concentrate on providing as many examples as possible of assessment and recording techniques. All the examples used have been tried and found useful in the classroom. We believe that the material in this chapter is valid not only to meet statutory requirements but also to support and enhance pupils' progress during the learning process.

There will be a particular focus on formative assessment, teacher observation, classroom testing, peer assessment, self-assessment, which all contribute to the pupils' development. In our opinion the more pupils are involved in assessing and recording their own attainment, the better their progress.

The purposes of assessment

We assess for a number of reasons:

- formative: to enhance motivation by making assessment a part of the continuous learning process;
- summative: to give pupils feedback on their attainment at a particular point in time. This is often conducted formally;
- informative: to give pupils, parents, other teachers and others feedback;
- diagnostic: to monitor individual needs and help identify special educational needs;
- evaluative: to select, order pupils and, if appropriate, identify levels of attainment and check the effectiveness of our teaching.

The assessment cycle

It is possible to conceive situations such as very formal examinations, when teachers are assessing without teaching anything, but impossible to imagine a situation when one is teaching without assessing in some way or other. Assessment must be seen as one step in a continuous cycle:

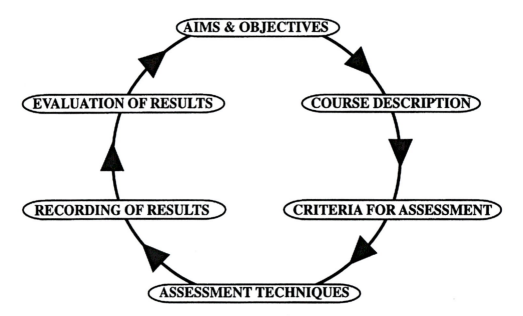

Figure 9.1

In other words, you have to know what you are going to assess before you work out the basis and the techniques for assessment, recording and reporting. The National Curriculum provides a basis for assessment. A department's scheme of work will have to offer much more detail and show smaller steps in the process of teaching and testing.

Assessment techniques

A simple mapping tool for the identification of assessment techniques would look as Figure 9.2.

Before we list examples of these techniques translated into modern foreign languages, a few comments are apposite.

When?

Linguists are, perhaps, too reliant on end-of-unit, end-of-course tests. They provide only part of the picture of a pupil and are particularly good at assessing recall, a vital, but far from the only, skill which we need to assess. They can lead

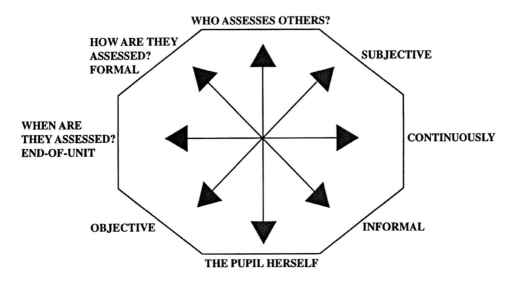

Figure 9.2

to teachers teaching towards the test, especially when many of the tests provided by coursebooks involve material not thoroughly covered in individual units of work. They are inappropriate tools on which to base National Curriculum levels, as National Curriculum statements are not applicable to individual pieces of work, but of work over a period of time.

Many of the teaching strategies we use in the classroom are also good assessment strategies and provide important evidence of attainment. The real answer to the question 'when?' is most likely 'All the time, in a variety of ways'.

How?

It would be unwise and unfair to denigrate the importance of formal assessment techniques, whether they be tests, internal or external examinations. Pupils need to get used to formal conditions and recall is an essential element of language learning. One can, of course, control the amount of support one gives a pupil, according to her needs. The most informal types of assessment include practical tasks and verbal and written comments on work by the teacher.

Who?

Assessment can be undertaken by the teacher, pupils themselves or peers, other adults, such as the FLA or older pupils. Teachers traditionally want to do all the assessment, a frustrating, well-intentioned, but misplaced, use of time. All agents can contribute to assessment, provided that clear criteria are given. Marking can be based on error counting, on interpreting performance criteria and on general impressions of quality, depending on one's purpose.

Pupils can be very astute and can handle and even create criteria such as accuracy, attitude, contribution to group task, behaviour, quality of work. This applies to all four language skills. This is not intended to undermine the importance of teacher assessment, which remains the cornerstone of teaching.

Subjectivity?

We are a little sceptical of the usefulness of multiple-choice and true/false techniques, even though they are now back in favour in the GCSE. Objective techniques are easy to mark, but they are difficult to construct and potentially boring for pupils. There are alternatives. Try ordering items, matching items, gap-filling, sentence finishing. The informality of unstructured role-plays and free writing activities may be difficult to assess, but they are close to the reality of the language activity of real life.

Some examples of assessment techniques

Though the four language skills are dealt with separately here, we acknowledge the fact that many of the tasks provided by teachers will combine more than one skill. Indeed, this is good practice. Many of the DfEE's Optional tests and tasks (SCAA 1996a and 1997) are constructed on this basis. Teachers can use the same task to provide evidence for more than one skill, as exemplified by the range of test activities identified for each skill or attainment target below.

1. Listening

- distinguishing between sounds;
- dictation;
- following the same text as a listening comprehension and filling gaps;
- compatible gapped texts in which each text has different words omitted for pupils to read to each other;
- listening comprehension, e.g. listening and ticking categories on a grid;
- drawing/completing pictures using taped/spoken text as a prompt;
- following instructions/directions;
- selecting appropriate pictures and colouring, responding to radio reports/TV/video (e.g. weather on map);
- ticking appropriate responses to spoken instructions.

Responses can combine with other skills, for example:

- writing notes in the target language;
- reporting orally what has been heard;
- answering questions on the heard text;
- filling in blanks/grids while, or after listening to, a text;
- putting pictures in order according to a story or text spoken by teacher;
- gapped script of telephone call (pupil invited to correct a badly-heard message on answerphone).

SCAA (1996b, p. 16–20) offers some early stage examples of how to test listening and record achievement.

2. Speaking

- role-play: structured (pupils given explicit instructions of what to say) or unstructured (pupils given general scenario of the situation);
- pronouncing individual words;
- reading aloud/reciting text/poem/passage;
- retelling stories;
- speaking from picture prompts;
- finishing off a sentence;
- comparing pictures;
- guessing what the people in the picture, on the muted TV screen are saying;
- carrying out interviews with or without cassette;
- conducting surveys;
- passing on a telephone message;
- asking questions;
- performing playlets or sketches assessed by partner, teacher, group or class;
- giving talks or one-minute presentations on a topic;
- taking part in a group discussion;
- carrying out group oral assignments;
- training pupils in the use of criteria to assess each other's oral work.

Recorded examples of ways in which speaking can be assessed can be found in a range of publications, for example SCAA (1996b, pp. 21–2).

3. Reading

- multiple-choice testing of vocabulary;
- true/false answers;
- matching items (for example, words to definitions or phrases to pictures);
- completing sentences;
- filling gaps with grammatically correct items;
- cloze procedure;
- carrying out written instructions to complete a task (for example, drawing something, making something, folding something);
- reading a text and identifying or showing understanding of individual words or the gist of the whole passage.

Again, tasks can combine with other skills, for example:

- taking notes on a passage read;
- using reading as a stimulus for writing;
- completing a form;
- reading a message prompt to assist with speaking on the phone;
- following written instructions or directions to mark a diagram, plan, map.

4. Writing

- rearranging a text in the correct order;
- blank-filling;
- sentence or paragraph completion;

- form-filling;
- note-taking (guided or free);
- notes expanded into free writing;
- free writing with criteria for assessment (essay/story/account/letter);
- writing from picture stimuli (photographs, cartoons, a picture series);
- answering written questions in the target language;
- summarising in writing;
- copy writing;
- creating a text/message on a word processor;
- amending a model;
- error recognition and correction (editing some written text and re-drafting).

5. Integrated assessment tasks

- taking part in a group practical task (for example, preparing correspondence for an exchange visit);
- designing something and producing it (a 'topical' page of a school newspaper);
- solving a problem (a written puzzle, to be discussed in the target language and outcomes written up);
- listening to a text, writing notes about it, then preparing and delivering a spoken summary (for example about someone's daily routine).

The National Curriculum

There are many documents you may consult to get the latest information on the statutory requirements for assessment. The only reminders we choose to give in this work are as follows:

- Teacher assessment is of paramount importance as it is the only source of evidence of progress over the duration of the period of compulsory and post-compulsory education. It gives teachers an element of control and provides immediate feedback for pupils.
- Schemes of work should plan in clear opportunities to assess. This implies that schemes refer to each attainment target and indicate assessment opportunities.
- Teachers should devise a simple, manageable recording system. A simple record for each pupil over Key Stage 3, such as the one in Figure 9.3, is a valuable method of tracking pupils annually from Year 7 onwards. This should be for internal use for the department. In this example, the internal record is in terms of levels. We can see little advantage and potential damage if pupils or parents are given levels any more frequently than the Qualifications and Curriculum Authority (QCA) recommends: once – at the end of Key Stage 3 (QCA/DfEE Statutory Assessment at Key Stage 3).

PUPIL RECORD CARD   **LANGUAGE**

NAME   BEGINNING 2000

Year	AT1	AT2	AT3	AT4	Lang
7					
8					
9					

Figure 9.3

Self-assessment

It is common sense to state that the more a pupil is responsible for her own assessment, the more understanding there will be of what is required and the more determination to deliver it. If self-assessment is desirable, how can teachers facilitate it? The answer may be in taking the time to train pupils in the appropriate techniques and in negotiating and understanding the appropriate criteria. Nevertheless, self-assessment is an imperfect art and is not as successful or as convincing as peer-group assessment. Someone else's critical eye can always pick up errors and qualities which self-assessment can miss. Various approaches have been found to work:

(a) If the task is clearly described, the criterion for success will be whether or not the pupil has carried it out as described, entirely on his own, whether or not support has or has not been required in the period leading up to carrying out the task. The pupil works on a task with a partner and assesses whether or not he has carried out the task and the teacher verifies this on a random sampling basis, as she moves about the room.

(b) Criteria can be created for a writing task. The pupils can be asked to assess for accuracy, presentation and imagination. Even if the criteria are not broken down into detail, it is surprising to see how seriously and maturely pupils will take to the task. They usually prove to be severe judges of their own work.

(c) Answer sheets can be provided for the kind of task which is right or wrong. The example in Figure 9.4 was created by a group of Tameside teachers as one of a pack of materials for use by non-specialist supply teachers. Pupils were expected to mark themselves in order to spare the teacher on her return to work. As a pupil completes a task, she takes an answer sheet, easily created by the teacher, and checks her work.

Look at the 6 members of an identity parade. Read the statements and tick the box if it applies to each of the people. Put a cross if it does not apply.

	a	b	c	d	e	f
Er ist groß						
Er ist sehr groß						
Er ist klein						
Er ist dick						
Er ist schlank						
Er raucht						
Er hat einen Hut an						
Er hat einen Pullover an						
Er hat eine Jacke an						
Er hat einen Mantel an						
Er hat eine Krawatte an						
Er hat eine Brille an						

Figure 9.4

From these examples it is already clear that pupils need prompts in order to assess their own work. The time spent in providing them is well worthwhile and saves hours of needless marking afterwards.

How do we deal with error if a child is assessing his own oral work? This will only become a problem if self-assessment is the only form of assessment employed. It would be unwise to rely significantly on self-assessment. The teacher should sample work in progress by moving about the room, occasionally with a clipboard for recording. By making the pupil responsible for her own recording, which the teacher will be able to countersign on a regular basis, the teacher will decrease her own workload and gain powerful allies in the pupils themselves.

Those that are not skilled in self-assessment will still move a little towards the skills the teacher is trying to develop. Remember, you are not opting out! You will still work on accuracy with the appropriate pupils at appropriate times. It is inappropriate to concentrate on accuracy all the time.

The computer can be used as a source of data for pupils to consult: answers, models and guidance for other assessment activity such as example dialogues. A word-processing package can be used to record the vocabulary required for particular tasks, to provide examples of answers to questions on a text, examples of letters to be written. Pupils will be able to refer to such information when they need to, in order to check what they have done independently of the teacher.

Peer-group assessment

In many ways similar to self-assessment, peer-group assessment has added social and support benefits. It can be a powerful element of formative assessment. In classrooms where, in these days of straightened school funds, special educational needs support is not always available, particularly at Key Stage 4, other pupils may provide a willing and friendly alternative to teacher assessment and/or pupil failure to cope. Pupils are sometimes much better at explaining than their teachers and may be less intimidating, provided that the teacher has made it clear to them that the aim of the exercise is to support and not to threaten or humiliate each other. The importance of positive comment should be stressed. Children are resilient to the comments of their peers. Nevertheless comments such as 'That's rubbish!' do little for confidence and may cause some pain.

The speaking task in Figure 9.5, can be carried out and assessed in pairs. It is taken from the Tameside level 1 graded objectives materials for German. In this and the previous section we have chosen examples for the productive skills as these are the ones which teachers are often sceptical about for peer-group and self-assessment. Another benefit of peer-group assessment is that it can help with class control. By inviting a class to help in assessing role-plays, for example, pupils are occupied and get up to less mischief while their classmates are performing.

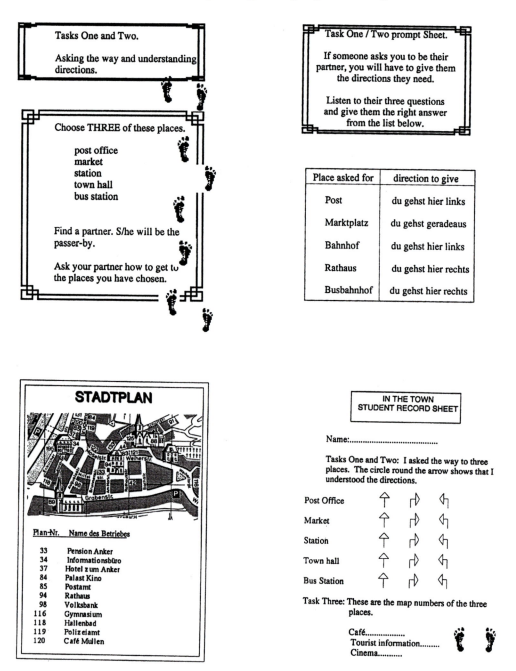

Tasks One and Two.

Asking the way and understanding directions.

Choose THREE of these places.

post office
market
station
town hall
bus station

Find a partner. S/he will be the passer-by.

Ask your partner how to get to the places you have chosen.

Task One / Two prompt Sheet.

If someone asks you to be their partner, you will have to give them the directions they need.

Listen to their three questions and give them the right answer from the list below.

Place asked for	direction to give
Post	du gehst hier links
Marktplatz	du gehst geradeaus
Bahnhof	du gehst hier links
Rathaus	du gehst hier rechts
Busbahnhof	du gehst hier rechts

STADTPLAN

Plan-Nr.	Name des Betriebes
33	Pension Anker
34	Informationsbüro
37	Hotel zum Anker
84	Palast Kino
85	Postamt
94	Rathaus
98	Volksbank
116	Gymnasium
118	Hallenbad
119	Polizeiamt
120	Café Mullen

IN THE TOWN
STUDENT RECORD SHEET

Name:.............................

Tasks One and Two: I asked the way to three places. The circle round the arrow shows that I understood the directions.

Post Office

Market

Station

Town hall

Bus Station

Task Three: These are the map numbers of the three places.

Café..................
Tourist information.........
Cinema............

Figure 9.5

Standardisation

If end-of-unit or end-of-course assessment are to have any significance beyond your own classroom, you will have to arrive at some agreement with colleagues in your own school and, perhaps, beyond it. The processes involved have a direct relationship with the assessment cycle already discussed and with the strategies appropriate for the 'levelling' of pupils required by the National

Curriculum. We believe that the strategies we describe here are valid ways of bringing together the thinking of a group of teachers, whatever the statutory requirement may be.

Schemes of work must relate to the National Curriculum Attainment Targets and indicate assessment opportunities as each group progresses through an academic year. This will enable you to ensure that you cover the programme of study across each Key Stage. Occasionally teachers should audit the tasks they set to check that they offer pupils of all abilities the chance to reach their full potential. If all tasks set are 'closed', this can be very limiting.

Once a year, it may be useful for teachers in a department to meet together to create or add to the departmental portfolio of pupils' work. This portfolio could initially contain the work of three or four pupils of different abilities. In each case a small number of samples of work for each language skill, particularly writing and speaking (the more contentious skills as far as assessment is concerned), would be discussed and related to the National Curriculum levels, with the teachers arriving at a consensus and giving a level at which each pupil is consistently working for each skill and for the language concerned. In one brief session a department should be able to produce examples of pupils working at three or four levels. Over a three-year period, if this process is repeated, a portfolio will accumulate examples of pupils working at each level.

QCA (formerly SCAA) has provided exemplification materials and sets of optional tests and tasks (SCAA 1996b). These are not intended to be benchmarks for the levels or the only method of assessment; they are, however, useful indicators of thinking at a national level. They provide some excellent examples of how to assess all four skills, with examples in a range of languages.

Teachers can only gain in time and quality of work by sharing materials, cross-marking, observing and helping each other.

Marking written work

In language teaching, there is little that is more soul-destroying than marking poorly written scripts, especially if the focus of attention is solely on accuracy. If the end result of one's efforts is a script covered in red ink, the problem lies in the nature of the task set, the preparation for its completion and your decision to use a colour which most pupils find threatening, even when your comments are positive.

Writing in a foreign language is inevitably troublesome to a large number of people. So, if we move pupils from presentation to free writing without sufficient practice and guidance, many fruitless hours will be spent pointing out errors rather than confirming success. One way of mitigating failures of accuracy is to point to success in communication, with positive credit and comments given to language that communicates effectively despite errors.

Of course, pupils' work has to be checked regularly. Error recognition and correction have a significant part to play in learning a language. In the early stages of developing writing skills, guidance should be such that pupils can generally succeed. This may mean practice in copying (preferably not from the board), gap-filling, sentence completion, imitating a model paragraph.

Pupils need training to acquire the mechanics, so that they can approach the process of writing with confidence. It is important to take the fear out of writing. Pupils marking their own work (or that of peers) is often a useful procedure for providing immediate feedback, time for correction and new opportunities for learning. It is also perhaps the most efficient and formative way of marking reading and listening activities done for non-test purposes in the classroom.

For pupils' own understanding and security, a common departmental marking policy is advisable. This may include flexible arrangements indicating that at times pupils will be marked for one feature only, for example past tense forms, genders, politeness (whatever the metalanguage used to explain the purpose). If everything is marked, the learning potential is sometimes diminished. When the focus is on one particular issue pupils can be asked to check their own work (or that of peers) before handing it in, potentially reducing the hard-pressed teacher's burden. This approach is controversial and may be considered a risk by some teachers. It is certainly worth considering, as present practices seem so unproductive for many pupils.

On the other hand, for more advanced learners, we may decide at times to mark everything. Whatever the policy, pupils should be clear about the method and purpose of marking. In a sense, the principle of gradually diminishing support operates with greater accuracy expected of pupils the more they are exposed to the language. Clear indications of what will be closely scrutinised will make misunderstanding less likely when feedback is given.

An agreed system of error indication helps pupils to develop a sense of what to look for and for some this probably aids learning. This will include abbreviations but they must be explained to the pupils, as their meanings are not self-evident, for example:

Sp., T., WO., Vb End., Adj. (Selling, Tense, Word Order, Verb Ending, Adjective)

In addition to error recognition, positive recognition of achievement is vital. The following descriptions have a part to play in showing appreciation for pupil efforts:

Bien communiqué	*Bien fait*	*Bien écrit*
Intéressant	*Ton travail m'a plu.*	
Excellent	*Bon travail*	*Super, etc.*

Such comments, however, do not give pupils the feedback which will move them on. From time to time a detailed comment on strengths and weaknesses gives them a written record to refer to. This may happen only now and then, as it is time consuming, but we can envisage instances when this is a valid and meaningful alternative to detailed or even selective marking of a piece of work or series of pieces. The decision whether to write this in the target language or in English must be left to your judgement. If pupils have difficulty in understanding it, it will have little, if any, impact.

If expedient and acceptable to pupils, red ink is best avoided particularly if there is a policy of getting learners to look at and review their own work. The use of a pencil means that those pupils who are motivated to correct can rub out your markings when they review and correct the work. In any case, red is seen by most pupils as a negative, aggressive colour. If asked, many may tell you that they prefer green.

Crucial to teacher success and well-being is the avoidance of endless hours spent on unfocused marking, a laborious task that eats into time that would be better used for preparation. Easing the burden is possible by providing immediate feedback and correction in the classroom, by marking for one key feature (usually the current teaching point), by asking pupils to review and check certain forms before submitting work; such strategies are legitimate aids to learning.

One technique observed by one of the authors involved the teacher at Key Stage 4 simply underlining selected key sentences in pupils' books. In the subsequent lesson, she elicited the underlined sentences from six or seven pupils in order to create a coherent text, wrote the sentences on the board and invited the class to work together in small groups to 'improve' each sentence (by correcting it or altering the style or register). During the course of a term, all pupils had the opportunity to have their work edited in this way. They worked together to improve their work; a fair copy was created on the board for copying as a model into exercise books. This is a useful way to organise feedback.

Marking oral activities

It is less easy to mark oral activities or indeed give as much individual feedback, although experiments have been conducted in Tameside and elsewhere with self-assessment in group oral assignments. Pupils were asked to grade themselves against a given set of criteria after completing oral tasks with their peers. Samples of teacher grades and pupil grades showed a surprising rate of agreement between what the teacher perceived and how pupils felt about their performance. In some, there was a tendency to under-rate their effort but peers would generally contest these 'over-modest' assessments. The use of group oral assignments is certainly valid and motivating for pupils as well as being a time-saving alternative to the one-to-one interview. It prepares classes for the demands of the one-to-one oral but in a less threatening and more supportive framework.

Recording progress

A simple and accessible method is required so that a department can quickly respond to requests for information. The traditional mark book is still the best expedient. It may be useful to set out the record for each class to indicate progress against the four Attainment Targets. There is no reason why this should be in terms of 'levels'; simple marks are very informative. The levels of attainment can be recorded for internal use annually during Key Stage 3. An example has been shown in Figure 9.3.

Whatever the system, the widest possible consultation and consideration is necessary to make sure that the system is both user-friendly and adequate for the needs of the National Curriculum.

Evidence

The assessment techniques identified in this chapter provide a wide range of evidence of assessment. At present there is no statutory requirement to retain evidence in order to justify judgements made on pupils' progress. Indeed, the prospect of retaining vast amounts of material such as end-of-unit tests or individual cassette recordings would be a nightmare to the majority of teachers and cause untold storage and retrieval problems. However it is essential to base teachers' judgements on evidence. Evidence can be termed primary or secondary.

Primary evidence is the actual outcome of a task – a piece of written work, a labelled diagram, a cassette recording, a video, a photograph of a performance, a model. One of the best pieces of primary evidence is the pupil's own exercise book or folder. It is not really practical to retain much primary evidence. The portfolio of assessed work already described is the closest most teachers may get to this.

Secondary evidence will usually be in the form of a record of some kind. It could be an account by the pupil or the teacher of what happened, a mark or grade in a record book, a log book, a checklist of pupils' names with all the tasks indicated on it, duly ticked and signed by a teacher. A major factor in teachers' relying on secondary evidence is that it occupies less storage space than primary evidence.

In the past too little confidence was placed in teachers' assessments of their pupils' progress. It is now clear that subjective professional judgements, particularly if exercised in relation to some form of standardisation, can provide a good basis for assessment.

A record of the activities undertaken by a class or an individual pupil will offer a great deal of evidence of attainment, as many tasks are assessed on the basis of successful completion as the only criterion of success. The amount of support that individual pupils need in order to carry out a task varies.

Pupils with special educational needs will need support from a variety of sources:

- peers (in pairs or groups);
- the language teacher;
- the design of worksheets;
- prompts which summarise the task simply;
- the type of language used by the teacher.

The following task was designed for pupils with learning difficulties. It would, of course, be explained by the teacher:

Shopping for clothes – how would you ask for one of the following items?

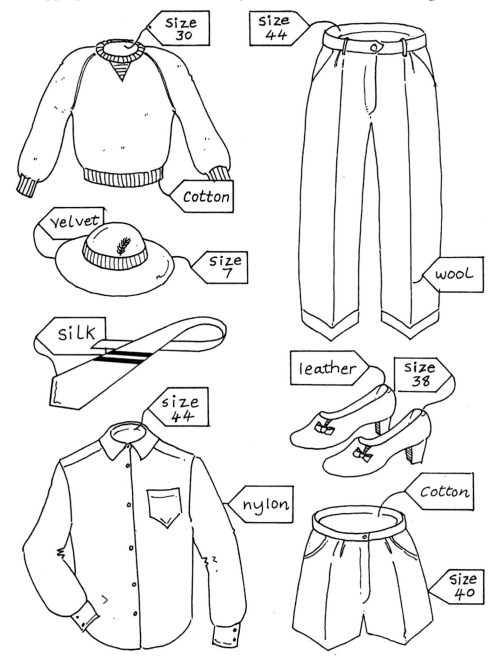

Figure 9.6

Integrated assessment tasks

Language does not naturally work in separate skill compartments. Assessment tasks can combine or even integrate the language skills, as noted earlier.

The classroom can be set out to become a resource base, with the teacher as facilitator rather than expert, and the pupils working under their own initiative to solve a problem. This was the basis of several Technical Vocational Education Initiative (TVEI) courses around the country in the 1980s. For example, the class can be invited to work in groups on a scenario in which the teacher is the 'boss' of a firm which is establishing links with its equivalent in Germany or France. The groups will carry out a series of tasks which will provide information for the links and discover and use the target language appropriate for the job. Assessment will then be of individuals' contribution to the group and of tasks related to the four language skills. Much of the assessment can be carried out by the pupil herself or by peers.

Target-setting

Records of Achievement influenced classroom practice in the 1980s and 1990s. Though they, perhaps, overstressed the place of records (and caused many a forest to be felled), they equally highlighted the importance of the process of target-setting and reviewing. It is logical good practice to involve pupils in target-setting and to work with them to review progress.

Rather than attempt to offer a comprehensive guide to target-setting, we shall restrict ourselves to showing ways in which you can avoid making the process an administrative nightmare.

1. Use the exercise book or the pupil's folder where you can.
2. Avoid comment banks, the so-called timesavers. They can cause more trouble than they save and predetermined phrases should not be applied to describing individual effort and achievement.
3. Give the pupils prompts to help them identify their personal targets. The following example presents pupils with ideas which will have to be confirmed by the teacher:

Figure 9.7

4. Use a whiteboard and adopt a whole-class brainstorm approach to negotiating targets. For example, if the topic is 'my house', you can work out the language they will need to know and the tasks they will need and wish to carry out by a process of class discussion.
5. Reviewing needs to take place once only each term or even less frequently. It need not be undertaken on a one-to-one basis, but can be done with the whole class, using the board, or in pairs or groups, using prompts.
6. Cross-curricular reviewing can be a good motivator and can demonstrate the links between modern foreign languages and other areas of the curriculum.

Organisation and Planning

Here is a set of prompts for organisation and planning which were part of a document produced by a group of Tameside teachers with one of the authors:

Your statements

I always/usually/sometimes

- plan my work well
- plan in advance
- meet deadlines
- keep my homework diary up to date
- leave homework/coursework to the last minute
- find it difficult to plan ahead
- bring the correct equipment to class
- arrive at my lessons in time
- attend school regularly
- keep my file/exercise book up to date and well organised
- can find my work easily in my file
- take care over the presentation of my work
- have found out what matters most
- know how to target my efforts on what matters most.

Similar prompts were created for personal and social skills, study skills and problem-solving and reviewing.

Assessment and recording are an area of work which teachers find worrying and for which, in our opinion, there is a lack of practical advice. We have attempted in this chapter to provide some ideas and examples.

Section 5: Foreign languages post-16

Chapter 10

Teaching modern languages at A/S and A Level

Students bring a lot with them when they enter sixth-form study to prepare for AS or A Level examinations. They have, to various degrees, been successful in their GCSE examinations; they are enthusiastic; they have experience of language learning situations, they may have experienced the target language country and the culture first hand. Hopefully, they have made an informed choice and want to learn more of and about the language. Linguistically, they are able to perform a range of transactions in the foreign language and they probably have good listening skills in the target language, some awareness of the features of the target language culture and a knowledge of everyday vocabulary. It is a reasonable foundation on which to build, given that their classroom experience of learning the foreign language has been somewhere between 350 and 400 hours.

The challenge

Typically, an A/S or A Level course will involve the development of the four skills so that interaction in the target language is done with ease. As a result, students should be able to:

- engage in sustained use of the language for communication;
- put forward arguments and discuss ideas, attitudes and opinions in the target language;
- demonstrate knowledge and understanding of contemporary culture and institutions in a target language community.

This will mean that students can listen to and read extended pieces of language in different registers from a variety of sources and respond to them, orally or in writing, clearly and accurately in the target language. The examinations at AS Level reflect an oral/aural bias, the 1999 A/S Level being a 50 per cent part of the A Level. For Associated Examining Board (AEB) AS Level, students do an oral (20 per cent) and a listening, reading and writing paper (30 per cent). They are required to complete tasks in all four skills.

At A Level, the patterns of assessment vary across examination boards but the balance tends to be the same, for example: the present NEAB examination consists of a reading and writing test (40 per cent), a listening test (20 per cent) an oral (20 per cent), coursework or a final written paper on Culture and Society (20 per cent), based on prescribed texts and topics; the AEB examination consists of a listening, reading and writing test (30 per cent), a reading and writing paper (30 per cent), a topics paper or coursework (20 per cent) and an oral (20 per cent). While the organisation may be different, each skill area has an equal weighting. When choosing the coursework or final paper (on topics related to contemporary society, recent history or literature) the preferences of staff and students can be taken into account. It would be better to teach literature with enthusiasm than teach something more 'trendy' such as modern cinema when the teacher has little interest it.

In the sixth form, linguistic expectations are high and the workload demands are heavy. Students need to build quickly on their GCSE foundation to become pro-active independent learners who are able to think critically about their own learning. The skills and knowledge that they need to develop go well beyond the transactional, to enable them to apply their language skills in ever wider contexts and in relation to more challenging topics. One would also expect that sixth form study would afford them opportunities to develop greater intercultural understanding and greater ability to explain the language (its grammar and vocabulary) in an explicit way, using appropriate metalanguage.

To achieve this kind of competence, learners will need guidance on the development of organisational skills:

- organising their work,
- planning for tests,
- understanding and acting on the demands of the syllabus,
- managing their time, and
- planning their development over an extended period;

and specific study skills, such as:

- reference and research skills,
- learning how to use resources such as the library and the Internet,
- reading for learning,
- memorising new vocabulary,
- taking clear notes,
- revising regularly.

For some students, these skills may already be in place, for others the learning curve will be quite steep. Pachler and Field (1997, pp. 336–41) provide a useful summary of the differences between GCSE and A Level in terms of functions, topics and grammar. Many students will have covered the topics: house and home, personal and social relations, shopping, travel and transport. But, in the sixth form, they will be expected to use the target language to focus on problems of the environment, unemployment, dangers facing young people. There is an expectation that students will be able to discuss and write in an informed and balanced way about contemporary social problems, race relations, political conflict and other issues that may be of interest to young adults. Despite the difficulty of bridging the gap, students often show surprising ability to produce in the target language, as shown by Jones *et al.* (1993), when three lower sixth form students produced impressive and moving poems about pollution in French.

The gap may seem wide, but students do bridge it. Sensitive and sympathetic, yet rigorous, induction to sixth-form work helps to bridge this gap. We recommend that the task be approached from a positive appreciation of what students already know and attention has been given to the issue. There are resources developed that seek to address the so-called gap (for example, Pillette 1998). The Objectif Bac course (Pillette and Clarke 1999) seeks to integrate a 'bridging the gap' element into its first level. Thorogood and King (1991), Pickering (1992) have also provided useful guidance for teachers working at this level. Barnes and Powell (1996) consider the need to develop high-level reading skills (including literature reading), exploring the skills involved and making practical suggestions.

We recommend that sixth-form studies begin with an initial assessment of the four skills to achieve a profile of competence. The demands of the A Level can be discussed with students who need to be made aware of the cultural knowledge, vocabulary and grammar needs of the syllabus. The implications are that teachers will need to offer differentiated approaches to plug the gaps as they occur; they may not be the same for each student. Usually, a topic-oriented approach seems to be preferred with scope for work on the four skills, grammar and vocabulary acquisition, and supplementary materials to stretch the more able and plug the gap for others. In addition, consideration needs to be given to the development of study skills and independent learning, so that students are aware of what is expected of them and what support is available to guide them in their choices.

General methodology for post-16 studies

Ideally, all activity will take place in the target language, though there may be occasions when a first language explanation could prove useful, for example, to explain the formation and use of the subjunctive or Past anterior in French. Where a translation component is still part of the course, then a bilingual approach is inevitable. Otherwise, the aim should be total immersion by the end of the first term, with tolerance for error but an increasing focus on accuracy. A thirst for the intricacies of the language should be encouraged and appreciated.

The style of teaching in the sixth form may be less formal, depending on the context and the teacher. The room could be laid out in seminar rather than traditional classroom style. Relationships between participants may be different with learners seen as researchers for their own learning, the teacher as the prompter and organiser, offering opportunities for student to follow up on areas of interest (through further reading and searching for materials in the Internet, for example).

The tasks and methods used in the sixth form often follow the patterns already discussed in earlier chapters. The teaching of reading and writing continues with pre-reading and pre-writing activities focusing on brainstorming for ideas, generating responses to the topic being studied, working on key vocabulary and exploring the different genres of the language. Information gap activities may still be used and occasionally there may be games, though these should be linguistically challenging, generating the use of lots of language (not just fun). Problem-solving tasks should play a greater part as should intensive listening and reading of texts. Greater assistance than at pre-16 levels may be needed to organise the acquisition of vocabulary with regular check-tests to make sure the burden is being evenly spread. Students should be encouraged to gather phrases from their reading and experiment with them in both speech and writing.

Grammar practice

A range of classroom-based activities can be used including question–answer work, analysis of texts, pattern practice, sentence reorganisation and completion. It is impossible to explore more than a few examples. For focusing on grammar, the cloze text approach is useful as shown by Rinvolucri (1984). Students are given a text with every seventh or tenth (or eleventh) word missing and they have to decide what can go in the spaces. Sometimes, the choice will be restricted to one possible answer only. At other times, there may be several possibilities and discussion should ideally take place in the target language about the choices made. The gaps may be shown in the text or they may be hidden. A more challenging variation on this activity is to provide a text with random grammatical items missing (one per line, but not content words) and students have to work out not only what is missing but where it goes. For example, a text presented along the following lines does not have the missing items indicated by spaces, making it into a correction exercise:

1. *Le 11 août 1999 midi, une éclipse de soleil a plongé une partie de la France*
2. *et de l'Europe une brève mais extraordinaire obscurité. Un grand*
3. *ruban noir large d'une centaine de kilomètres recouvert pendant deux*
4. *minutes les villes Cherbourg, Fécamp, Dieppe, Rouen, Amiens,*
5. *Compiègne, Laon, Metz, Strasbourg, puis partie de l'Allemagne, de l'Autriche et de la Roumanie.*

   (text adapted from an article by Jean-Marie Homet, in L'Histoire **233** Juin 1999)

The missing words are: *à* (line 1) before 'midi', *dans* (line 2) before 'une brève', *a* (line 3) before 'recouvert', *de* (line 4) before 'Cherbourg', *une* (line 5) before 'partie'.

Putting together jumbled text can also be useful, if the re-constitution involves recognition of grammatical and semantic links and relationships, for example this text from the opening paragraph of Chapter 2 of *Le Silence de la Mer* (Vercors 1944). Students are asked to collaborate in ordering strips of text into the paragraph whose beginning and end appear in the middle of the page without italics here below:

Ce fut ma nièce qui . . .

J'étais assis au fond de la pièce, relativement dans l'ombre

alla ouvrir quand on frappa

court un trottoir de carreaux rouges

Ma nièce me regarda et posa sa tasse

Elle venait de me servir mon café, comme chaque soir (le café me fait dormir) sur le jardin, de plein pied

Tout le long de la maison

très commode quand il pleut

le bruit des talons sur le carreau

Nous entendîmes marcher

La porte donne

... Je gardai la mienne dans mes mains.

Through the above, rules of agreement and possessive pronouns can be explored as well as expressions such as *donner sur, venir de*. The strategy is one that can be applied to any text, even poetry.

Dictation can also be used very creatively. Instead of a straightforward transcription of what the teacher reads aloud, partial dictation (with gaps for the learners to fill in according to their understanding) can also be used. In addition, 'dictogloss' (Wajnryb 1990), the task of reconstructing a spoken text in the learners' own words, is also a possibility. Dictogloss has a clear four-stage methodology:

1. Pre-dictation stage: students are prepared for the important vocabulary and content of a short text.
2. Dictation stage: students hear the text twice and during the second listening make brief notes of key words and the main ideas.
3. Reconstruction: students, in groups, work together to re-build the text from their notes, with teacher as monitor.
4. Analysis and correction: students analyse and improve their texts, with sentences pooled on a board or OHT for discussion; or they can simply compare their text to the original, the aim being to achieve a gloss, a version which has the same meaning as the original, not necessarily identical words.

Apart from being interesting and fun to do, these exercises also force the learners to interact more with the meaning of the dictated text, to make sense of it and produce meaningful language. This collaborative exercise helps to create a positive, supportive atmosphere where learners at any level can explore the language. For a full account of creative approaches to dictation and examples, you are recommended to Wajnryb's work (1990).

In some courses, translation may be a feature, for example in the present AEB syllabus where translation into English is a requirement and in NEAB syllabuses, translation into the target language and into English still feature. Translation is a practical skill and occasional practice of this is valuable. It does not have to be dull, as variations are possible:

- quick translation activities of two sentences, the results compared among students;
- translating a short text into English then back-translating into the target language to see if the original can be re-constructed;
- listening to and translating from the spoken word.

Translation often has a communicative purpose and as a small element of the syllabus and methodology, it is justified. Its use in the classroom is helpful to develop explicit grammatical and lexical knowledge. The results of a translation can also be discussed in the target language.

Skimming, scanning and extensive reading

One of the principal challenges facing sixth form learners is the development of rapid reading skills. These can be encouraged in the classroom by providing opportunities for quick activities, for example offering the students a pile of news sheets (perhaps from *Authentik*, Trinity College). Each student selects an article and writes one target language question on a slip of paper. The slips are collected and redistributed. Students then have to skim and scan the available articles to find the answer to their question.

Articles can be distributed without their headlines, then students match headlines to articles. They can be asked to read one article and then write two sentences which capture the main idea(s) beginning:

Cet article s'agit de . . .

For guidance on strategies to develop reading, Grellet (1981) and Nuttall (1982, 1996) offer excellent ideas that can be used at this level, for example:

- reading and answering key questions,
- reading for specific items of information,
- reading and transfer of information to a chart, form, table, or picture,
- reading and performing a task.

It is important to avoid slipping into a similar approach (often an intensive exploration of the text) of reading for each lesson to maintain a balance of skimming (for gist), scanning (for specific information), intensive (for detailed understanding) and extensive reading (for recreation or extension).

Encouragement should be given to students reading longer texts (journals, newspapers, short stories). This can be done in relation to the coursework or topic-work element where this takes place, for example reading of the copies of topic-related magazines. For instance, a 1999 copy of *L'Histoire* (no. 233, June 1999) featured articles on the French Resistance in the Second World War. Of course, the reading of publications which deal with issues of topical interest (sport, fashion, current affairs) should also be encouraged, as should newspapers (some, such as *Le Monde* are available on CD-ROM). Textbooks now offer a vast amount of reading material suitable for learners provided they are helped not to feel overwhelmed. Topic-related materials have also been developed (for example, publications containing articles from *L'Express* magazine, by Steele (1999) and Steele and Paris (1994). CD-ROMs can also play a part (for example, the Collins series, Autolire, CD-Lectura, CD-Lesen). Rapid gist reading followed by quick oral question–answer activity can help to make the task more manageable and success-oriented. Key questions could be selected from the following:

- *De quoi s'agit ce texte en général?*
- *Est-ce qu'il y a un problème? des problèmes? Quel est le problème?*
- *Qu'est-ce qui arrive? Qu'est-ce qui est arrivé? Pourquoi?*
- *Quelles sont les conclusions?*
- *Que pensez-vous à ce sujet?*

or the equivalent in the target language.

Quick reading of texts can help students with vocabulary acquisition by providing experiences of words and phrases beyond classroom activities, helping to sensitise them gradually to usages and frequent collocations. The development of independent habits of reading is critical to success at this level and continuing improvement not only in language but also in knowledge about the target language culture and community.

Writing

Understanding of varied types of writing is required at A Level, meaning the understanding of a range of genres and forms of writing (reports, articles, poems, novels, e-mails). While the essay is the dominant genre in many syllabuses, other forms of writing should be supported. It can be difficult to work out how sixth-form coursebooks seek to help the development of writing. It is worth taking the time to analyse the advice they give on the process involved and the types of writing expected. In many cases they provide topic-related opportunities for the writing of articles, letters, summaries, posters and essays (for example, in *Au Point* by Deane *et al.* 1994). However, it is important that teachers organise writing activities in a supported and guided way so that students have opportunities for planning, drafting and re-drafting. In our view, the key to the successful teaching of writing lies in the pre-writing preparatory phase when students review the topic, generate ideas and plan the writing. Students need guidance on the process of writing: on the need for a clear purpose, the need to keep in mind the audience for their writing, and to establish a clear coherent focus on the topic of their writing. Then, a decision can be made on the form that the writing should take, how it should be organised. Models of how other people have written can be analysed to help students appreciate what goes in a report, in an article, a protest letter, a summary, a review; how these forms of writing open and close, what they typically contain. An example of this approach to analysing a model can be seen in *Au Point* (p. 15) in relation to agony aunt mail. Attention has been given to providing help with the demands of essay writing at advanced level, for example *Aufsatz! 2000* (Hares and Clemetsen 1998) and *Compo! 2000* (Hares and Elliot 1997). Textbooks and dictionaries provide examples of how native speakers write similar texts and often use these as stimuli for writing.

The Internet can provide support to learners so that they can write on areas of topical interest and enhance their work with illustrations (maps, photographs, drawings) as with the following text. This article, done as a homework exercise, drew on information found in French newspaper reports and links to the *New*

York Times website. It was submitted with a map of the crash site, a photograph of the coastline and photographs of the victims of the air accident drawn from Internet sources.

John Kennedy junior disparaît en mer

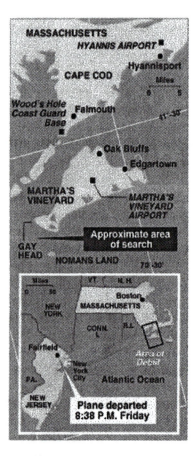

Encore une tragédie pour la famille Kennedy! John Kennedy junior, fils du président américain tué le 22 novembre 1963 à Dallas, a disparu hier au large des côtes du Nord-Est des États-Unis. Des bateaux et des hélicoptères ont mené des recherches pour retrouver le petit avion. La gendarmerie maritime a déjà trouvé un morceau de tapis, un repose-tête et une valise sur une plage.

John Kennedy et sa femme ont quitté l'aéroport de Fairfield, à l'ouest de New York, vers 20h30 (heure locale). Les radars ont détécté l'avion. Un peu après, John Kennedy a annoncé par radio son approche finale à l'aéroport de l'île. Soudain, à une vingtaine de kilomètres de sa destination, l'avion a disparu des écrans radars.

Le président Bill Clinton a été informé tôt samedi matin de la disparation de John Kennedy. Il a déclaré: "Toutes nos prières et nos pensées sont avec les familles de ceux qui se trouvent à bord de l'avion."

Né le 25 novembre 1960, John a fait de longues études de droit. En 1996, il s'est

marié avec Carolyn Bessette, 28 ans, fille d'un médecin de New York. John Kennedy avait passé son brevet de pilote l'année dernière.

Figure 10.1

Coursework

It is in the area of coursework where students are perhaps most challenged to broaden their horizons and their approach to study. Opportunities will be found to deploy research skills:

- looking for source material (paper, video, electronic) of a variety of types and styles,
- seeking help and guidance from overseas contacts via e-mail or letter,
- using the Internet and encyclopaedias (possibly CD-ROMs) to find additional information,
- using monolingual dictionaries.

Depending on the choice of topic (the literature option often offered a more straightforward focus for planning and resourcing) teachers will need to make sure that adequate resources are at hand. Study boxes and catalogued topic files filled with press cuttings, photographs, reports and photocopies of documents are an effective resource for coursework elements. The provision of up-to-date journals may also be a requirement, for example, for the topic '*L'Année 1999 en France*', a weekly newspaper (perhaps *Le Monde*), the journals *Le Point* and *Les Clés de l'Actualité* could be considered. Lack of space forbids a more detailed discussion of the possibilities, but access to such material can be gained via the Internet and through the purchase of CD-ROMs and published materials (for example, *Authentik*). Contacts with cultural representatives (Austrian Institute, Goethe Institut, Institut Français du Royaume-Uni, Italian Institute, Instituto Cervantes) are helpful in securing up-to-date resources. For guidance on sources of available material, or on any aspect of language teaching, the Centre for Information on Language Teaching (CILT) in London is the most informative and helpful contact.

Successful coursework requires the maintenance of momentum and interest so that application is continual, leading to final submissions that reflect the ability and commitment of the learners concerned. Endless dabbling with coursework resources is not the answer; a planned focused exploration is what is called for. This is easier when the topic is a set literature text, though the response to literature study is often less enthusiastic.

It is worth recalling that although students are required to study the society and culture of a target language community, in most syllabuses this accounts for 20 per cent of the total examination syllabus. While teachers need to be very well-informed to be able to support the coursework element, they also need to keep a sense of perspective, making sure that the general A Level course progresses alongside the coursework. As Pachler and Field (1997) observe, A Level teaching is often shared and it takes up no more than six hours of the timetable in any week. Careful coordination and teamwork are required if the programme is to be delivered in a balanced comprehensive way. Independent learning is essential to success, but successful teachers at this level regularly monitor what their learners are doing, advising on time management and study skills. With supervision, students are able to complete the topic and coursework elements without damage to the development of other parts of the programme.

If literature is chosen as part of the coursework or topics element, a range of target language tasks to complement or prepare for essay writing can be used to help students, as shown by Wicksteed (1993). Her suggestions include gap-filling, mime, role-play, acting out scenes from novels. Such strategies can be used so that the literature experience is not just one of wading through difficult text.

In this chapter we have touched on the issues facing the sixth-form teacher of languages to AS and A Level. Inevitably, we have only been able to scratch the surface, outlining the challenges and suggesting some strategies. As A Level studies change after the year 2000 in order to offer students the chance to study more subjects, the current extensive demands should moderate. However, we are confident that post-16 students will still have to develop the skills to:

- become independent critical learners,
- acquire a balanced competence in the four skills,
- communicate with ease in speech and writing, using appropriate grammar and vocabulary,
- use metalanguage to describe and analyse the language they are learning,
- acquire an appreciation of some aspects of the target language community, its institutions and culture (including, where it is chosen for study, some literature).

This is what language learning is about and we hope that with modifications to 16–19 expectations more students will be persuaded to opt for what is a life-improving opportunity.

Section 6: Information and communications technology

Chapter 11

Using ICT in modern languages – an introduction

Many teachers have mixed feelings about the use of information and communications technology (ICT). It offers teachers and pupils a wide range of stimulating, motivating ways of developing and practising language skills. It can easily, however, become an obsession and dominate the thinking and approach of the teacher. It is noticeable that OFSTED inspectors often criticise the lack of ICT in departments. This is sometimes given greater prominence in reports than other aspects of classroom practice and may reflect a misplaced faith in the magic of technology. Basically, we consider it a useful teaching aid with as many strengths and weaknesses as other teaching aids. For instance, the computer can be used to develop reading skills with Internet sources or by exploring databases.

There can be no doubt that the potential of this particular teaching aid is significant. It motivates pupils of all abilities. Able pupils like to work independently and the computer allows them to work apart from the teacher. Disruptive pupils are often calmed by the computer and will get on with their work. Less able pupils can gain access to foreign language learning by using various pieces of software or hardware. Teachers can create tasks drawing on all four language skills, though there is no doubt that there are fewer activities which involve oral skills than there are for the other skills. Information retrieval and word processing are still the principal uses made by language teachers. As software, particularly voice-active software, becomes more easily accessible and more successful in its design, language teachers will find many more uses for the computer.

Unfortunately, many teachers may be wary of the computer and lack the skills and confidence to make full use of it in their teaching. Equally, many schools are unable to offer full access to the computer to language teachers. The constant complaint is that they cannot get time for their classes in the ICT room. Both of these situations seem set to change in the near future. The National Grid for Learning (NGfL) has set a number of targets for teachers and pupils to be achieved by 2002. Hardware is becoming increasingly cheap to buy. Substantial amounts of funding have been set aside for training teachers and financing the purchase of software and hardware. The New Opportunities Funding training is likely to have a significant impact on classroom practice. As more technology becomes available, there will be greater integration of Internet resources. Inevitably, ways will be found to increase the number of computers and computer rooms in schools. E-mail, for example, will soon become part of the everyday currency of learning. The Internet is already a generous source of ideas for teachers and materials for pupils in all languages taught in the UK.

Pupils' entitlement to ICT

The current National Curriculum for modern foreign languages has a number of elements which can be addressed by the use of ICT. Pupils are expected to:

- communicate in the target language;
- communicate with people in target language countries;
- develop in all four language skills;
- enhance their language learning skills;
- enhance their independent learning skills;
- have access to a range of resources in the target language;
- have their special educational needs met to give them access to modern language learning;
- make effective use of ICT in the development of the four skills.

Although ICT is inevitably a statutory element of the National Curriculum for all subjects, some aspects of the national curriculum for ICT cannot easily be delivered in a modern language lesson. Other applications, however, support the fundamental aims of modern languages, for example communicating and handling information is a particularly important element of the ICT curriculum which is our business. In addition, pupils can learn to adapt and present information in a variety of ways, using the computer to combine words, numbers, sound and pictures and to present them in a manner suitable to the purpose identified by the teacher or some other audience.

Varied audiences are, in fact, a major motivating factor for pupils. A disenchanted 15-year-old might well be motivated to produce something worthwhile, even accurate, for a pupil of the same age at the other end of the world or for a tourist visiting his or her home town. Pupils can also handle information on the computer: access, store, retrieve, present and adapt all types of information, whether they be factual or not.

There is, however, an equal opportunities dimension to the issue of computer use and computer access. The current lack of access to computers which some departments experience should be resolved as the NGfL has its effect but there are other issues, for example: uneven levels of teacher skill and confidence could result in pupils experiencing differing degrees of involvement with ICT; some, but not all, pupils will be able to do homework and additional coursework on their computers; boys may often dominate in the computer room in mixed gender classes.

Classroom organisation and ICT

The two environments which can be a setting for the use of ICT are the specialist language classroom and the ICT room. At present modern language teachers find it difficult to gain access to the ICT room, which is usually dominated by the teachers of ICT, maths and science, with English somewhere in the wings. Hopefully, this will change as schools create three, four and more ICT rooms and, in many instances, locate banks of computers in language rooms.

Modern foriegn languages in the languages specialist room

One of the problems with relying on the computer in the specialist room is that it can become the focus of the whole lesson, with pupils waiting for their 'turn', doing 'less important' tasks until they can move to the computer. This attitude does not seem destined to change, as pupils become more and more accustomed to the presence of IT in their lives. It never seems to become boring and is a perpetual magnet. The obverse also happens, with the exasperated teacher deciding to leave well alone and leave the computer neglected and unused in a corner of the room. Much depends on the skill of the teacher and her knowledge of what can be done with a stand-alone computer in the classroom. There are ways of integrating the computer into lessons. The situation would be even better if there were a bank of three or four computers in the specialist room.

The carousel approach is one method some teachers employ. For example, a series of lessons can be planned for an able Year 9 group on the topic of healthy eating. The activities in the carousel could be:

- writing a list of different kinds of foods, identifying which are healthy which not (word processing, desktop publishing);
- role-plays that simulate interactions in various departments of a store in which the pupils become a family or group of friends discussing what to buy from the point of view of healthy eating;
- listening to a taped interview with a food expert and answering questions based upon it;
- writing an article for a French newspaper on healthy eating in England (leading to word processing or desktop publishing, or e-mailing attachments to partner schools);
- working on the computer to create a database of various foods and their nutritional value with a view to making recommendations for school dinner policy. This could involve looking at foods sold in the school canteen and their nutritional value. They could in turn be compared to those of a school overseas and the diet there.

The stand-alone computer can be used to support pupils with learning difficulties, freeing the teacher to move around the class to offer support to a greater number of pupils. Word processors can be used to create simpler versions of a text or task or offer word banks, word lists for some pupils to refer to.

The concept keyboard, for which many commercial courses now provide materials, can be used with pupils with moderate learning difficulties. Changing the colour of the background screen on a computer is a technique used to help pupils with specific learning difficulties (dyslexia).

There are CD-ROMs of dictionaries which can be made available throughout a lesson. The Internet can be accessed for individual research on topics covered in lessons, the environment (Canadian sites offer texts on *la couche d'ozone* which were used by the student who completed the work shown as figure 11.1) health-related issues (*la drogue, le SIDA*), third world issues. For sixth-form topic work, the possibilities are limitless.

Of course, the computer can also be used as a 'treat' for pupils who have done particularly well.

La couche d'ozone

La couche d'ozone, qui est le seul écran solaire naturel de notre planète, se trouve dans la haute atmosphère terrestre. Elle agit comme un filtre invisible qui protège toutes les formes de vie contre les dangers de la surexposition aux rayons ultraviolets du soleil.

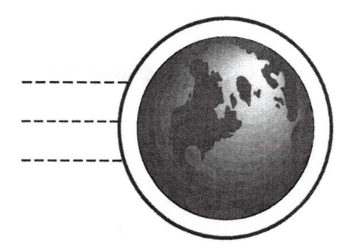

Figure 11.1 Examples of sixth form work

L'appauvrissement de la couche d'ozone

L'appauvrissement de la couche d'ozone mène à la surexposition aux rayons ultraviolets du soleil, et cela provoque des cancers de la peau. La couche d'ozone mince ne peut pas absorber les rayons ultraviolets du soleil.

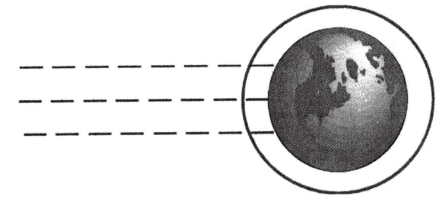

Qu'est ce-que c'est la cause du problème?

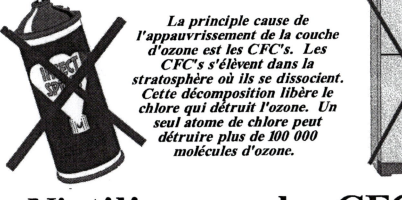

La principle cause de l'appauvrissement de la couche d'ozone est les CFC's. Les CFC's s'élèvent dans la stratosphère où ils se dissocient. Cette décomposition libère le chlore qui détruit l'ozone. Un seul atome de chlore peut détruire plus de 100 000 molécules d'ozone.

N'utilisez pas les CFC's !

Figure 11.1 continued

Modern foreign languages in the ICT room

Schools are increasing the number of ICT rooms at a rapid pace. There will soon be many opportunities for modern languages teachers to take their charges into an ICT room. Ideally, large networked rooms will set out to enable the class to move away from the computers for a more conventional teaching approach for part of the lesson. A whole lesson at the computer can easily be filled, but its merits as a good use of time are debatable. Half the lesson at the computer may be sufficient to do what is needed. Indeed, determining when it is appropriate to use the computer is a key element in the training of teachers to enhance teaching and learning, as acknowledged in the specifications for providers of New Opportunities Fund training.

One of the main dangers to be encountered in an ICT room is not that computers have a tendency to misbehave at inappropriate times, but that pupils can spend a whole lesson without speaking or even hearing a word of the target language. The computer, after all, is at present more easily used for writing and reading than for listening or speaking. You should try to give instructions in the target language during the lesson. BECTa provides comprehensive lists in many languages to assist you in this.

Software for modern languages

There are literally hundreds of pieces of software dedicated to modern foreign languages. Unfortunately, only a small number appear to be successful, but there are many generic applications of ICT which enhance teaching and learning: simple word processors can be employed to adapt a text; pupils can 'edit' a text by changing the person, the number or the tenses of the verbs; adjectives and adverbs can be added to enhance a text.

There are a number of items of text manipulation software, such as *The authoring suite* (Wida Software), and *Fun with texts* (Camsoft). There are also some sets of games which replicate the computer games many pupils play at home, but place them in a modern languages environment. These include *Ten out of ten* (Didactic) and the sets of French, German and Spanish games (*Dix Jeux Francais, Zehn Deutsche Spiele*, and *Diez Juegos Españoles*) produced by AVP. In 1999 the most popular and successful pieces of software, in addition to the ones mentioned, included *All-in-one Language Fun, Triple Play Plus* (Syracuse Language Systems), *En route, Unterwegs* (Granada Learning) and *Who is Oscar Lake?* (LPI) All of these can be recommended (see p.192 for details), but they are counter-balanced by hundreds of pieces of software of questionable value.

The Internet

The Internet is a dynamic, ever-changing source of ideas and materials for teachers and resources for use with pupils. With this in mind, we do not consider it appropriate here to name many individual websites, as they are born and die almost daily. It is, however, appropriate to mention a small number of sites dedicated to modern languages teaching. BECTa have many links to modern languages on their site (http://www.becta.org.uk). The Association for Language Learning (ALL) has its own site which is developing a wide information base for teachers (http://www.languagelearn.co.uk). Another useful site is Ling@net (vtc.ngfl.gov.uk/resource/linguanet). Each of these sites links with many other sites of interest, including web pages created by pupils. Searching the web can produce a treasure trove of resources and ideas.

It is now relatively easy for pupils to create their own web pages. The software needed is usually provided free by service providers in browsers such as Netscape Communicator or Microsoft Explorer. The latest versions of word processors usually have the facility to create web pages.

E-mail, if properly managed by the teacher, motivates pupils to write and undertake other language work for audiences which are a change from their own teacher, 'real' audiences. Townshend (1997) offers useful guidance on the use of e-mail in foreign language teaching. Topics they can draw upon include:

- pocket-money survey results
- pop music
- meals and food
- our town
- my holidays
- parents' jobs
- book reviews
- captions for cartoons
- greetings cards
- local menus
- news comment
- questionnaires
- sports.

(adapted from Townsend 1997)

The Internet also has discussion groups for older pupils, some 'live'.

Working with the computer

You should never hesitate to ask yourself whether the computer or a particular piece of software is being used for its own sake. There are definitely occasions when the computer can get in the way of your aims, because of the amount of time it can take up and the frustration it can cause when one is led from link to link, with no real information gathered. It can be used to develop and practise all four language skills, though speaking and listening activities are more difficult to find than writing and reading. ICT is useful for grammatical work, background material and project work. It is in the latter that the most sophisticated uses of the computer in modern languages can be identified. ICT coordinators look to project work for the higher levels of the national curriculum for ICT, as pupils can combine multimedia, Internet, desktop publishing and other computer facilities to display imagination and initiative. For example, a Key Stage 3 project could be created on the topic of computer games in the home country and abroad. Through the web, classes could be contacted in a number of Spanish speaking countries. The joint project could be to look at the range of computer games available in each country and compare information. Pupils could create a web page with scanned-in pictures of the software adverts, their descriptions of how they work and a review of each piece of software described. They could include links on the page to their own e-mail addresses and useful websites.

They can send software by snail mail (or the web, if it is shareware or freeware) for receiving classes to sample and compare notes on. Each class can then produce a piece of writing to be e-mailed, giving reactions to the software tried. They might even create a new advert in the target language, using clip art and photographs to advertise the product in the receiving country.

The Internet is becoming an essential tool for advanced level students. It can be used to access the day's newspapers and magazines, the latest news, both in exclusively written form and items broadcast on the web with visual and audio materials. It provides an encyclopaedia of up-to-date background knowledge for students to use in their essay and coursework.

An increasing number of publications and many sites on the web make a thorough exploration of the topic for which this chapter can serve only as a brief introduction. The possibilities for the enhancement of teaching and learning are significant, provided that ICT applications are chosen and used appropriately.

Section 7: Conclusion

Chapter 12

Finding the time

Teachers have too often received poor press coverage. They are easy scapegoats for society to blame for perceived shortcomings in pupils' attainment. Certain parts of the press would have it that there are many unskilled teachers who are unable to give their pupils a good education. In general, we have had difficulty finding many such teachers.

Sadly, however, there are a few whose work may be characterised by some of the following failings:

- laziness
- dislike or intolerance of children
- lack of praise
- failure to put the child at the centre
- unwillingness to consider or seek alternatives
- tolerance of chaos in the classroom.

Those who consistently work against the interests of their children match what the public might call the 'bad teacher'. The children recognise them quite easily. Poor modern language teachers are guilty of not marking, not preparing, taking easy ways out without considering the needs of the pupils, not using the target language when it should be used, failing to control classes and not setting or not marking homework. But for the loss of education and other damage done to their children, such cynically inert teachers would merely be a sad irrelevance in the classroom. In our experience very few fall into this dire category.

We have, however, observed some teachers struggling with a very heavy workload and limited resources. It is not surprising that in such circumstances staff may not match up to the high standards that they set for themselves, slipping into practices that diminish the effectiveness of foreign language teaching:

- getting out of the habit of promoting the target language
- not taking account of learner needs, for example by doctrinaire use of the target language when it is clearly unhelpful
- not incorporating sufficient variety
- always using the same strategy (e.g. role-play)

- being unwilling to try other ways of teaching
- not considering how pupils might learn
- failing to exercise positive discipline in the classroom.

Combating these dangers and maintaining a fresh enthusiastic approach is not easy at times when teachers are deluged with paperwork and constant change. Teacher stress is now acknowledged as a major source of absenteeism and illness. Workload, lack of clear information concerning school and national agendas, relationship difficulties (pupils, colleagues, senior management) all contribute to teachers' insecurity and overload. Some easing of the burden is possible to avoid the extremes of the workaholic, on the one hand, and the bad teacher on the other. Dealing with relationships and information problems are not necessarily in the hands of the teacher, though wise managers do their utmost to alleviate these.

Planning for the language classroom

Despite pressures of workload and time, careful planning of learning outcomes saves much frustration for both teacher and learner. This need not be complicated, with the process of detailed reflection intermittent rather than continual. It may take the form of a simple plan to assess the successes achieved in the classroom:

Class	Time	Unit
Teacher Activity	**What the pupils learn**	
Evaluation		

Figure 12.1

The format does not have to be restricted to one lesson. It could be used to reflect upon the achievement of one unit or indeed to measure the targets set for a group over a period of time. Did the teacher do what was planned? What kind of learning took place? Answers to questions of this nature will determine the targets to be set for future development. The review can be done with the pupils, going on to explore learning techniques described in Chapter 6.

Such a process may also help to identify which learners need to learn different things in different ways. An instance of this would be the realisation that some learners would greatly benefit from an input on grammar, while other learners may learn more effectively through practical activities. Without such a reflective process it is difficult to see how individual learning differences can be addressed and appropriate action taken. Some teachers reflect on the interactions that have taken place in their classrooms: which pupils they have spoken to directly in a given week, who has used the target language in the classroom, how much pair and group practice has been organised, who has submitted written work and who has not. Such reviews help teachers to follow up on lapses and plan for the inclusion of learners in opportunities to develop language skills.

When measuring achievement in the classroom, it is helpful to have an accessible record of lessons. Some mark books include space for this type of record which can be very helpful in the planning and preparation of schemes of work.

Teachers may benefit from a list of criteria against which they might review performance and then draw up an action plan. This may include language specific issues:

- setting clear objectives for language learning;
- presenting language clearly;
- using the target language;
- giving instructions in the target language;
- providing for a balance of skills (LSRW);
- using the textbook creatively;
- consulting pupils about their preferred language-learning techniques;
- pacing practice appropriately;
- using the cassette or video recorder appropriately;
- producing language learning materials;

as well as issues of importance that apply to any reflective teacher:

- organising pair or group work;
- using the board clearly and effectively;
- using the OHP;
- incorporating ICT to assist learning;
- helping pupils to learn (strategies, support, suitable homework);
- controlling the class;
- giving genuine praise;
- generating interest;
- evaluating pupil progress;
- providing equal opportunities for learners of all abilities;
- marking; and
- enjoying the job!

Such a checklist may serve to guide individual teachers and departments as they prepare for departmental reviews, appraisal meetings, inspections or interviews. A small number of the categories above may be chosen as a focus for development of one or more members of staff.

Time for reflection

Another feature of importance that has probably suffered from recent pressures is the issue of time for evaluation of one's work in the classroom. Assuming that excellence in the classroom is the goal, time to consider objectives and reflect upon successes is surely a valid demand. Departmental meetings might devote more time to this, though the sad fact is that 'business' all too often gets in the way.

At any rate, we suggest that reflection be a part of the teacher's action plan as it can help avoid the type of overwork that is of no real benefit to anyone. Certainly, the gains from sharing issues with just one other person are immense – opportunities to bounce ideas and comment, to be listened to by a friendly ear and also to listen. Knowing other people's priorities and concerns can sometimes save a lot of work and time.

Classroom effectiveness

Research into school effectiveness appears to have recognised that a key determining factor is the quality of learning in individual classrooms. It is individual departments and teachers, more than whole schools, that have the most significant impact. The following eleven features identified as being characteristic of effective schools (Sammons *et al.* 1995, p. 8) are recognised as being crucial and some of them can also form a framework for the evaluation of one's own work within language departments:

- professional knowledge of the leading professional;
- shared vision and goals;
- a learning environment;
- concentration on teaching and learning;
- purposeful teaching;
- high expectations;
- positive feedback and reinforcement;
- the regular monitoring of progress;
- raising pupils' self-esteem;
- home–school partnership;
- a learning organisation in which school-based staff development takes place.

In our view, successful teachers

- have a will to communicate;
- explain things well and in interesting, sometimes funny, ways;
- know all pupils' names, care about them and get on with them, never patronising them;
- trust their pupils and seek to build them up (encourage them with positive feedback);
- show genuine enthusiasm for the job;
- know their stuff and reflect on how best to teach it;

- maintain high standards of behaviour and manage to maximise the amount of class time which is devoted to learning.

These may seem like high expectations, but we believe that it is what a large number of teachers achieve. Perhaps we should bear these ideals in mind as we do our best to develop skills, but also bear in mind that such expertise does not happen overnight.

Management of time

When setting objectives for ourselves we may usefully divide the week/month/half-term into blocks of time to be allocated to preparation, marking, lessons and other duties. At times, the balance may shift but it is unreasonable to give every waking hour to the job as many linguists appear to do. At the beginning of a unit of teaching, more time may be required for preparation and planning, while towards the end more time is absorbed in marking assignments or assessments and recording success.

The bane of endless documentation has come to clog the working lives of staff who would generally prefer to get on with teaching. There are few constructive options available though a lot of the paper would be best recycled. As electronic documentation becomes increasingly the norm, with teachers and schools having easy access to web-based sources and e-mail, this may become even more intrusive. Sharing the burden among colleagues may help, but this option depends on the size and interests of the department.

Sub-contracting chunks of reading to interested colleagues is one way of using resources economically, with colleagues providing a brief written or oral summary. Some local advisers summarise documents either through their own endeavours or those of working parties. Use these services as often as possible.

A strategy which may help you to cope with bureaucratic overload is to sort the tasks you have to do into three categories – A, B, or C. The As are the top priority which absolutely have to be done. The Cs are very low priority. Next, re-allocate your B tasks to either list A or list C. Then, if you are very brave or incautious, bin the C tasks. If you are more cautious put them away for a few weeks until nothing happens. Then bin them.

Other useful strategies are:

- write down reminders;
- set strict deadlines for completion of administration;
- handle paper only once, move it on to its destination or recycle;
- do not carry paper endlessly around in your briefcase or in the back of the car;
- live happily with the fact that you cannot do everything.

Resources

Many teachers spend a considerable number of hours (well beyond the 1265!) creating materials for their pupils. This was justified in the 1970s and early 1980s when existing approaches and materials were found to be unsuitable for many children who in the past would have been denied the opportunity of learning a language. The production of materials is often very satisfying but it can also become very burdensome and detract energy and attention from other important tasks such as planning units of work and setting clear objectives for lessons.

To ease the burden it is quite legitimate for staff to share both resources and resource-making tasks. There is no virtue in re-inventing the wheel. If appropriate materials can be bought then this frees teachers for preparation and rest. Commercially produced audiocassettes, videocassettes, computer software, flashcards and worksheets contribute significantly to successful learning programmes.

The selective and judicious use of textbooks is yet another valuable resource. We do not propose studying every page, but a flexible use of the book as a resource can make life much less fraught. Many learners also appreciate the value of a book. Some will even try to learn from it, especially when advised how to use it. A number of such courses have been mentioned in previous chapters.

In contrast, a sudden flight from textbooks can cause a lot of unfair late-night hardship to already over-burdened teachers. There are inadequacies in all published materials, but there is still a wealth of material that can help pupils learn. Many foreign observers are amazed at the obsession with materials production and at the conceit implicit in the belief that home-made worksheets will be free from all the inadequacies of published materials.

With regard to audio-visual aids (cassette recorders, overhead projectors, flashcards, whiteboards, flipcharts) the key to success seems to be in their flexibility and accessibility. Wallcharts are useful but limited. Flashcards are possibly the most useful visual aids for any age group. The OHP is versatile and ought to be in every classroom, provided that there is a good screen (or convenient bare wall) well positioned so that everyone can see. For quick presentations the chalkboard when well used is very effective. The cassette recorder has become a vital tool for presentation and practice activities. We are, however, increasingly aware that it is overused. Pupils all too often ask the teacher to repeat what the cassette has just told them. The disembodied voice is not necessarily a realistic source of spoken material. The cassette recorder should be used sparingly, especially during Key Stage 3. TV, video, ICT software and hardware are excellent supports to teaching and learning, but need careful planning for integration into language teaching activities.

It is essential not to be a slave to any one resource. Always standing at the OHP conducting activities will inevitably lose the attention of some pupils. An over-reliance on computers may leave pupils without adequate practice in listening and speaking. Technology is there to serve the needs of learners, which are not always perceived as matching the needs of the teacher. At times, pupils may find it simpler and more effective to work without complicated machinery, for example on sunny days, when they cannot read what is on the OHP because the classroom has no blinds or curtains! Not an irregular occurrence. All the resources are useful but we recommend variety and flexibility in the use of the different tools, as the teacher is still the most valuable resource.

Authentic materials

The use of authentic materials has become widespread in recent years and has been further facilitated by the availability of electronic sources of information. Reading and listening for meaning (for communication) are now well established beside the use of listening and reading for purely language learning purposes. However, an over-reliance on authentic materials may cause confusion in learners (as well as more unproductive late nights for teachers desperately recording radio snippets, scouring brochures and cutting up magazines, surfing the Internet, etc.).

Presenting 'undoctored' material may fail to take sufficient account of learner needs, particularly if bewildered pupils are asked to process raw speech. On the one hand, authentic materials are very useful for communicative practice purposes (e.g. train timetables, menus, newspapers, station announcements, recorded interviews) and occasionally for presentation (real objects, signs, posters from supermarkets, tourist offices, etc.). On the other hand, a doctrinaire insistence on their use may be counter-productive, as presentation of language generally requires some mediation by the teacher.

First language acquisition does not happen in an environment of unadulterated 'adult' language. Parents modify and simplify the language for their children. Teachers should not feel guilty when using non-authentic materials. Where authentic materials are appropriate and available, use them. Otherwise, use teaching materials (made by teachers) that help pupils learn. Learners themselves authenticate the materials particularly when they are seen to contribute to successful learning.

Valuing the task

The classroom task of the teacher of languages is the same privilege that it has always been – the chance to influence and observe the growth of language skills in young minds. Foreign language skills imparted to young people are a reason for celebration. When an activity is successful it is quite reasonable that a teacher should enjoy the moment and share the enthusiasm for learning with pupils. Such enthusiasm for children's learning is as welcome as the love of foreign languages.

Conclusion

Our expectations of our own work are sometimes left unsatisfied, but a reasoned evaluation of one's efforts may help to put things into perspective. Concentrating on what has been achieved in the 350–400 hours available to the compulsory language studied in the 11–16 curriculum is a first step to appreciating the measure of success rather than failure. Displaying negative responses to classroom work is not helpful to learners who require support and encouragement. After all, they have a lot more than language learning to contend with in their school life.

Despite all the frustration of unbalanced, adverse publicity and heavy workload, the practice of foreign language teaching in mainstream educational settings is a satisfying challenge because:

- teaching skills can be improved;
- children of all abilities are entitled to learn a language;
- children respond to praise, appreciation and success in learning.

To assure a fair measure of success in the classroom, we believe that:

- the learning of a language should be a positive experience;
- no one approach can provide learning for all;
- there is a place for up-front teaching, for active learning, for pair and group activities and for periods of quiet, disciplined work or study;
- authentic materials are not always essential;
- published materials are very useful;
- grammar and vocabulary are important elements in the development of the four skills (LSRW).

Finally, we believe that those who insist on a single method are probably misguided. The principal task is to build upon all the things that pupils bring to the classroom (personality, humour, knowledge, stories, learning skills, learning styles, qualities and needs) to involve them in a relevant and worthwhile experience.

References

Alder, J. (1997) *Developing Dictionary Skills in German*. London: Collins Educational.

Allen, V. F. (1983) *Techniques in Teaching Vocabulary*. Oxford: Oxford University Press.

Ashton, P., *et al.* (1982) *Curriculum in Action*. Milton Keynes: Open University Press.

Atkins, B., *et al.* (1995) *Collins Robert French–English English–French Dictionary*. Glasgow: HarperCollins.

Atkinson, T. and Lazarus, E. (1997) *A Guide to Teaching Languages*. Cheltenham: Mary Glasgow Publications with the Association for Language Learning.

Barnes, A. and Powell, B. (1996) *Developing Advanced Reading Skills in Modern Foreign Languages*. Cheltenham: Mary Glasgow Publications with the Association for Language Learning.

Barton, A. (1997) 'Boys' under-achievement in GCSE modern languages: reviewing the reasons', *Language Learning Journal* **16**, 11–16.

Bastian, S. and Best, A. (1987) *Borders, Layouts and Designs Book 2*. Blackwood: Alpha Visuals, Crucible Books.

Berwick, G. (1999) *The French Grammar File 11–14*. London: Longman.

Blagg, *et al.* (1988) *Somerset Thinking Skills Course*. Oxford: Blackwell.

Bourdais, D., Eaton, A., Sweeney, G., Rainger, A. (various) *Maxilire*. London: Longman.

Bourdais, D., Finnie, S., Gordon, A. L. (1998) *Equipe: Student's Book*. Oxford: Oxford University Press.

Briggs, L., Goodman-Stephens, B., Rogers, P. (1992) *Route Nationale*. Walton-on-Thames: Nelson.

Brown, S., Borgwart, S., Hampshire County Council (1996) *Deutsch? Kein Problem!* London: John Murray.

Buckby, M. and Corney, K. (1998) *Réussir à Lire*. London: Collins Educational.

Buckby, M., Jones, B., Berwick, G. (1992) *Learning Strategies*, London: Collins Educational.

Buzan, T. (1997) *The Speed Reading Book*. London: BBC Publishing.

Carle, E. (1969) *The Very Hungry Caterpillar*. London: Hamilton.

Colley, A. (1996) *Vu et lu*. Walton-on-Thames: Nelson.

Cook, V. (1996) *Second Language Learning and Language Teaching*. London: Edward Arnold.

Corney, K. and Buckby, M. (1995) *Vital 1*. London: Collins Educational.

Dakin, J. (1973) *The Language Laboratory and Language Learning*. London: Longman.

Davis, P. and Rinvolucri, M. (1988) *Dictation: New Methods, New Possibilities*. Cambridge: Cambridge University Press.

Deane, M., Powell, B., Armstrong, E. (1994) *Au Point*. Walton-on-Thames: Nelson.

Department of Education and Science (DES) (1989) *Modern Foreign Languages for Ages 11–16*. London: HMSO.

DES (1990) Modern Foreign Languages for ages 11–16. London: HMSO

DES/Welsh Office (1991) *Modern Foreign Languages in the National Curriculum*. London: HMSO.

DfE/QCA (1999) *Modern Foreign Languages – The National Curriculum for England Key Stages 3–4*. London: HMSO.

DfE/Welsh Office (1995) *Modern Foreign Languages in the National Curriculum*. London: HMSO.

Dirven, R. (1990) 'Pedagogical Grammar', (State of the Art article), *Language Teaching* **23**(1), 1–18.

Dobson, A. (1998) *MFL Inspected: Reflections on Inspection Findings*. London: CILT.

Dunning, R. (1997) *Cric Crac!: Teaching and Learning French Through Storytelling*. Clevedon: Multilingual Matters.

Ellis, G. and Sinclair, B. (1989) *Learning to Learn English: a course in learner training*. Cambridge: Cambridge University Press.

Elston, T., McLagan, P., Swarbrick, A. (1995) *Génial*. Oxford: Oxford University Press.

Finnie, S. (1993) *OK! Stage 1*. Cheltenham: Stanley Thornes.

Finnie, S. and Cambier, A. (1996) *OK! Stage 2*. Cheltenham: Stanley Thornes.

Finnie, S. *et al.* (1998) *Bouquins à la Mode*. Oxford: Oxford University Press.

Gairns, R. and Redman, S. (1986) *Working with Words: A Guide to Teaching and Learning Vocabulary*. Cambridge: Cambridge University Press.

Graham, S. (1997) *Effective Language Learning*. Clevedon: Multilingual Matters.

Grellet, F. (1981) *Developing Reading Skills: a practical guide to reading comprehension exercises*. Cambridge: Cambridge University Press.

Grenfell, M. and Harris, V. (1993) 'How do pupils learn? (part 1)', *Language Learning Journal* **8**, 22–5.

Grenfell, M. and Harris, V. (1994) 'How do pupils learn? (part 2)', *Language Learning Journal* **9**, 7–11.

Grenfell, M. and Harris, V. (1998) 'Learner strategies and the advanced learner: problems and processes', *Language Learning Journal* **17**, 23–8.

Grenfell, M. and Harris, V. (1999) *Modern Languages and Learning Strategies in Theory and Practice*. London: Routledge.

Halliwell, S. (1993) *Grammar Matters*. London: CILT.

Hares, R. and Clemettsen, C. (1998) *Aufsatz! 2000*. London: Hodder & Stoughton.

Hares, R. and Elliott, G. (1997) *Compo! 2000*. London: Hodder & Stoughton.

Harmer, J. (1987) *The Teaching and Learning of Grammar*. London: Longman.

Harmer, J. (1991) *The Practice of English Language Teaching*. London: Longman.

Harmer, J. (1998) *How to Teach English*. London: Longman.

Harris, V. (1997) *Teaching Learners How to Learn: Strategy Training in the MFL Classroom*. London: CILT.

Hewer, S. (1995) *Néothèque* (Reader Pack). London: Collins Educational.

Hewer, S. (1997) *Text Manipulation: Computer-based Activities to Improve Knowledge and Use of the Target Language. (CILT Infotech 2)*. London: CILT.

Holden, W. R. (1999) 'Learning how to learn: 15 vocabulary acquisition strategies', *Modern English Teacher* **8**(1), 42–7.

Hope, M. and Hunt, C. (1993) *Atelier Grammaire*. Oxford: Oxford University Press.

Horsfall, P. (1997) 'Dictionary Skills in MFL 11–16', *Language Learning Journal*, **15**, 3–9.

Jenkins, J. and Jones, B. (1991) *Spirale 1*. London: Hodder & Stoughton.

Johnstone, R. (1989*) Communicative Interaction: A Guide for Language Teachers*. London: CILT.

Jones, B. (1992) *Being Creative*. London: CILT.

Jones, B. (1995) *Exploring Otherness: An Approach to Cultural Awareness*. London: CILT.

Jones, M. G., Lynch, D., Beuzit, S. (1993) 'A-Level French: a case study of an intensive course', *Language Learning Journal* **7**, 36–41.

Kavanagh, B. and O'Connor, N. (1999) *Un Deux Trois*. London: Longman.

Kavanagh, B. and Upton, L. (1994) *Creative Use of Texts*. London: CILT.

Krashen, S. D. (1985) *The Input Hypothesis*. London: Longman.

Lanzer, H. and Gordon, A. L. (1995) *French Vocabulary Builder*. Oxford: Oxford University Press.

Lee, B. and Dickson, P. (1989) *Assessment in Action*. Slough: National Foundation for Educational Research.

Leicestershire Multicultural Resource Centre (undated) *Lord Rex* (ESL teaching resource).

Littlewood, W. T. (1981) *Communicative Language Teaching: An Introduction*. Cambridge: Cambridge University Press.

Littlewood, W. T. (1984) *Foreign and Second Language Learning: Language Acquisition Research and its Implications for the Classroom*. Cambridge: Cambridge University Press.

Littlewood, W. T. (1992) *Teaching Oral Communication*. Oxford: Blackwell.

Macaro, E. (1998) 'Learner strategies: piloting awareness and training', *Tuttitalia* **18**, 10–16.

Maley, A. and Duff, A. (1982) *Drama Techniques in Language Learning*. 2nd edn. Cambridge: Cambridge University Press.

Marriott, T. and Ribière, M. (1998) *Help Yourself to Essential French Grammar*. London: Longman.

Mary Glasgow Publications (1989) *Idées Pratiques Pour la Classe de Français*. Cheltenham: Mary Glasgow Publications.

Maslow, A. H. (1954, 1970) *Motivation and Personality*. New York: Harper and Row.

Matthews, A., Spratt, M., Dangerfield, L. (eds) (1985) *At The Chalkface: Practical Techniques in Language Teaching.* London: Edward Arnold.

McKay, S. L. (1985) *Teaching Grammar: Form, Function and Technique.* New York: Pergamon.

McNab, R. (1992) *Avantage: Book 1.* Oxford: Heinemann.

Miller, A. (1995) *Creativity.* Cheltenham: Mary Glasgow Publications with the Association for Language Learning.

Mitchell, I. and Swarbrick, A. (1994) *Developing Skills for Independent Reading.* London: CILT.

Morgan, J. and Rinvolucri, M. (1984) *Once Upon a Time: Using Stories in the Language Classroom.* Cambridge: Cambridge University Press.

National Council for Educational Technology (NCET) *Information Sheets.* Coventry: NCET.

Northern Examinations and Assessment Board (1998) *NEAB Italian Syllabus 1221.* Manchester: NEAB.

Nuttall, C. (1982, 1996) *Teaching Reading Skills.* Oxford: Heinemann.

O'Connor, N. (1998) *Help Yourself to Essential Spanish Grammar.* London: Longman.

Pachler, N. and Field, K. (1997) *Learning to Teach Modern Foreign Languages in Secondary Schools.* London: Routledge.

Pickering, R. (1992) *Planning and Resourcing A Level French.* London: CILT.

Pillette, M. (1997) *Effective Use of a Bilingual Dictionary.* London: Collins Educational.

Pillette, M. (1998) *Bridging the Gap in French at 16+.* London: Collins Educational.

Pillette, M. and Clarke, B. (1999) *Objectif Bac: Level 1 Student's Book.* London: Collins Educational.

Pincas, A. (1982) *Writing in English, Books 1–3.* London: Macmillan.

Place, D. J. (1997) '"Boys will be boys" – boys and underachievement in MFL', *Language Learning Journal* **16**, 3–10.

Price, L. and Semple, M. (1998) *Help Yourself to Essential German Grammar.* London: Longman.

Pye, J. (1989) *Invisible Children: Who are the Real Losers at School?* Oxford: Oxford University Press.

Rendall, H. (1998) *Stimulating Grammatical Awareness: A Fresh Look at Language Acquisition.* London: CILT.

Revell, J. and Norman, S. (1997) *In Your Hands – NLP* in ELT. London: Saffire Press.

Richardson, G. (1983) *Teaching Modern Languages.* London: Croom Helm.

Rinvolucri, M. (1984) *Grammar Games.* Cambridge: Cambridge University Press.

Rogers, P. (1999a) *Grammaire Directe.* Walton-on-Thames: Nelson.

Rogers, P. (1999b) *Grammatik Direkt.* Walton-on-Thames: Nelson.

Rogers, P. and Long, J. (1983) *Grammaire en Clair.* Walton-on-Thames: Nelson.

Rogers, P. and Long, J. (1985) *Alles Klar.* Walton-on-Thames: Nelson.

Rowles, D., Carty, M., Mc Lachlan, A. (1997) *The Foreign Language Assistant.* London: CILT.

Rubin, J. (1981) 'Study of cognitive processes in second language learning', *Applied Linguistics* **2**(2), 117–31.

Sammons, P., Hillman, J., Mortimore, P. (1995) *Key Characteristics of Effective Schools: A Review of Effectiveness Research*. London: Institute of Education for OFSTED.

Schools Curriculum and Assessment Authority (SCAA) (1996a) *Key Stage 3 Optional Tests and Tasks Modern Foreign Languages*. London: SCAA.

Schools Curriculum and Assessment Authority (SCAA) (1996b) *Consistency in Teacher Assessment – Exemplification of Standards in Modern Foreign Languages: Key Stage 3*. London: SCAA.

Schools Curriculum and Assessment Authority (SCAA) (1997) *Key Stage 3 Optional Tests and Tasks Modern Foreign Languages*. London: SCAA.

Slater, J., Coles, M., Paynter, T. (1987) *Borders, Layouts and Designs 1*. Blackwood: Alpha Visuals, Crucible Books.

Sprake, D., Rhymes, H., White, S. (1997) *Francoscope à la Mode*. Oxford: Oxford University Press.

Steele, R. (1999) *L'Express: Perspectives Françaises*. Oxford: Oxford University Press.

Steele, R. and Paris, J. (1994) *L'Express: Aujourd'hui la France*. Oxford: Oxford University Press.

Swan, M. (1985) 'A critical look at the communicative approach (part 1)', *English Language Teaching Journal* **39**(1), 2–12.

Swarbrick, A. (1998) *More Reading for Pleasure in a Foreign Language*. London: CILT.

Thompson, G. (1996) 'Some misconceptions about communicative language teaching', *English Language Teaching Journal* **50**(1), 9–15.

Thorogood, J. and King, L. (1991) *Bridging the Gap: GCSE to A Level*. London: CILT.

Tierney, D. and Dobson, P. (1995) *Are You Sitting Comfortably: Telling Stories to Young Language Learners*. London: CILT.

Tierney, D. and Humphreys, F. (1999) *Primary Storytelling Resource Pack*. Walton-on-Thames: Nelson.

Townshend, K. (1997) *Email – Using Electronic Communications in Foreign Languages Teaching*. London: CILT.

Trinity College, *Authentik Language Learning Materials*. Dublin: Trinity College.

Turner, K. (1995) *Listening in a Foreign Language: a skill we take for granted*. London: CILT

Ur, P (1984) *Teaching Listening Comprehension*. Cambridge: Cambridge University Press.

Ur, P. (1988) *Grammar Practice Activities*. Cambridge: Cambridge University Press.

Vercors, (1944) *Le Silence de la Mer*. London: Macmillan.

Wajnryb, R. (1990) *Grammar Dictation*. Oxford: Oxford University Press.

Wallace, M. (1982) *Teaching Vocabulary*. Oxford: Heinemann.

Wicksteed, K. (1993) 'Working with an A Level literature text: twenty-two ideas for target language activities', *Language Learning Journal* **7**, 17–18.

Wright, A. (1984) *A Thousand Pictures for Teachers to Copy*. London: Collins ELT.

Wright, A. (1995) *Storytelling with Children*. Oxford: Oxford University Press.
Wringe, C. (1989) *The Effective Teaching of Modern Languages*. London: Longman.

ICT Software

AVP: *Diez Juegos Españoles*; (Chepstow: School Hill Centre)
AVP: *Dix Jeux Français*; (Chepstow: School Hill Centre)
AVP: *Zehn Deutsche Spiele*; (Chepstow: School Hill Centre)
Syracuse Language Systems: *All in one language fun* (New York: Syracuse)
Camsoft: *Fun with texts;* (Cambridge: Camsoft)
Syracuse Language Systems: *Triple Play Plus* (New York: Syracuse)
LPI: *Who is Oscar Lake?* (Richmond: Talkfast International Limited)
Didactic: *Ten of ten* (Didactic)
Wida Software: *The authoring suite* (London: Wida software Limited)
Granada Learning Limited: *En Route* (Manchester: Granada Learning Limited)
Granada Learning Limited: *Unterwegs* (Manchester: Granada Learning Limited)

CD-ROMS

Collins Educational: *Autolire CD*, *CD-Lectura*, *CD-Lesen*

Index

3 5282 00634 1088

9 781853 465703